DESPATCHES FROM OLD TRAFFORD

a Red-Eye view of United 1993-1996

Richard Kurt

Published by Sigma Leisure – an imprint of
Sigma Press, 1 South Oak Lane, Wilmslow, Cheshire SK9 6AR, England.

British Library Cataloguing in Publication Data
A CIP record for this book is available from the British Library.

ISBN: 1-85058-559-8

Typesetting and Design by: Sigma Press, Wilmslow, Cheshire.

Printed by: MFP Design & Print

Cover Design: The Agency, Wilmslow

Introduction

"DESPATCHES FROM OLD TRAFFORD" is a comprehensive collection of journalism and writing by Richard Kurt, a pre-eminent chronicler of the modern United. Tackling every conceivable area of United interest in a unique style, the collection sums up the experiences of the Cantona Era – and with no apologies for the Great One's dominance. Supported by guest contributions from other terrace writers and artists, the book includes extracts from three books by Richard Kurt, his articles from national newspapers and magazines, some new profiles and, above all, his often acerbic contributions to Britain's best fanzine, 'Red Issue'.

Coming Soon, With Your Help...

Richard is keen to hear from any Reds who were around during "The Red Army Years" of 1974-86 and who would be prepared to be interviewed, anonymously if necessary, for the forthcoming book. Anyone who fancies writing a eye-witness piece about any aspect of those years – the aggro, the scandals, the fashions and the terrace heroes 'n' villains – is invited to send it in. All enquiries/offers please to R. Kurt, c/o Sigma Press, 1 South Oak Lane, Wilmslow, Cheshire, SK9 6AR.

You can also write to Peter Boyle at the same address if you wish to contribute to his forthcoming "Red Army Songbook": if you know any unusual United chants or songs, if you have any stories about great terrace choral moments, if you were there at the birth of a classic anthem or can even claim to have started one, Pete wants to hear from you as soon as possible.

Dedication

This book is dedicated to

Michael Hickey

whose struggle reminds us of football's true place

Contents

Part One:

THE NEWEST TESTAMENT - THE TRIALS OF LE DIEU

THE DIVINE INTERVENTION

Now we know precisely at what moment Fate changed course and sent us forward to claim the title. Leeds had phoned Martin Edwards to enquire about Denis Irwin, amusing in itself since the Sheep had had him on their books and dumped him. After Edwards had finished laughing, Alex prompted him to ask about Eric Cantona. 'OK then, he's yours' says Sgt. Wilko and the deal is done in a trice. A fairly ridiculous scenario to set up the most epochal transfer since Robbo's arrival over a decade before.

JFK's shooting had nothing on this. Where were you when you heard the news? Everyone can recall the shock, the joy and the pure *Scharden-freude* of that moment. Manc phone lines burned hot as the news spread whilst our Yorkie friends were paralysed by the trauma. Let us be honest: few of us had any real idea of what Eric was going to bring us – we may even have had nervous doubts. What was undeniable and utterly delightful was the knowledge that all Leeds would be devastated beyond endurance. The savage outbreak of recrimination, despair and anger in Sheep City was wondrous to behold. This was worse than Revie's death, worse than the '73 Cup Final, worse than your favourite ewe giving you an STD: all that could be heard from the East was the desolate howling of the betrayed lover.

I'd seen Eric play in France and had long been convinced that he was a Gallic George Best. When he came to England, I longed for him to come to OT but knew that Alex would never countenance such a presence in the dressing-room. I despaired when he settled in Leeds and fully understood the rapture of Elland Road as he unveiled his unparalleled majesty. Leeds fans, for so long the epitome of xenophobic macho-men, became homosexual Francophiles overnight. In a way this was not that surprising. Here was a player of thrilling flair, excitement and glitter-drenched individualism and thus as such was totally alien to Leeds fans; it was akin to showing primitive man fire for the first time. The Sheep duly warmed their genitalia on his incandescence on the pitch and me ... I felt as bitter as the most acerbic of Blues.

So as it turned out, there was no marriage between Leeds and Eric, just the briefest of affairs that left the Sheep impotent and frustrated. The spotty, shaven-headed Tyke fan had been granted a few nights with Kim Basinger and had fallen hopelessly in love only to watch in horror as she went off hand-in-hand with the hunk from down the road. Back to the local wildlife for Leeds – the start of a beautiful relationship for the Reds.

Why Eric left Leeds is a question shrouded in mystery and speculation. At the time, unsavoury rumours abounded which tended to refer darkly to 'off-the-field behaviour' – what Private Eye would term 'Ugandan discussions'. Certainly such stories kept *Red Issue* in jokes about donkeys, sex and housewives for months. When Eric's book came out, he accused Wilko of driving him out with his contradictory comments which left Eric bemused and uncertain of his standing. Wilko struck back in *The Sun* claiming Eric had forced him to sell and for a while legal action seemed possible. This wasn't even handbags at 10 paces – more pouting at 30 miles. Frankly, who cares? The French Genius, a supposed *enfant terrible*, became Eric the Red, King of Old Trafford and history was made. Leeds left with piles of Cantona Christmas presents – United left with a superstar, a title and a glorious future.

Perhaps the key to this is understanding that Eric is typically French. Anyone who's studied history knows that for France, glory – *La Gloire* – is all to them. Just winning is not enough; it must be done with style, panache and passion. Why did the French turn out to support Napoleon in such huge numbers when he came back from exile in Elba? Because they wanted glory, even if that meant glorious defeat. How could Leeds ever hope to fulfil this genetic need of Cantona? A club whose greatest moments are only remembered by the rest of the country for their cynicism, negativity, and 'efficiency'? A club whose recent title was won by default from a team they haven't beaten since 1981? A club so unused to flair or style that they left Eric on the bench more often than not?

Of course Eric came to us – who else in Britain can claim to have elevated true glory to the highest principle of living? Where else could Eric's existential vision be realised? Eric, an Albert Camus fan, would dismiss any notion of destiny but for those who believe in such things, how obvious that he should've ended up at the Theatre of Dreams. The Sheep were dreaming to think they could hold him there: Elland Road is the last place on Earth for a true artist. Now Brian Deane, well, THAT'S what I call Leeds style.

Dropping a sparkling star catalyst like Cantona into a team equation does not produce instant combustion, of course. The most perceptive early comment about Eric was from George Best who remarked that Eric had "given the team a brain at last." Naturally it would take a while for this new cerebral presence to mesh into the side, for it to link up the synapses and mainline into the team's nerve centres. You don't turn around teams in an instant – they're more like supertankers, gradually arcing around away from the destination marked 'More Aimless Bollocks' towards the port reserved for Champions. Even so, the rapidity with which United were transformed by Eric's arrival was surely without precedent in our history. We'd thought for months that we needed both a striker and a midfield player; now we had the two – but in one man. Both were the best in Europe.

(from the author's book 'United We Stood', Oct. 94)

THE RETURN OF L'ENFANT TERRIBLE

By autumn '94, the world was beginning to close in on Eric from all quarters. As he racked up the reds and yellows of wildly varying deservedness in England, the French too decided it was time to have a go. The count-down to Selhurst was accelerating ...

You'd think the French would have learned their lesson by now. Not content with hounding Eric the King out of their domestic league, it now appears that the press are determined to remove him from the national side too. Eric is being forced to endure a torrent of hacking onslaughts from his compatriots equal to that which he suffered at the hands of our tabloids last spring. The most disgusting aspect of this new affair however is that the press are dressing up what is essentially a clash of styles between Eric and the journos into an inquisition into Eric's personal character. Eric has never liked the hacks – now they have decided they don't like him either.

The root of all this angst and turmoil is, of course, the poor state of the French national team. A generation of fans brought up on the exquisite glories of Platini, Giresse and Tigana cannot cope with the return to the status quo of yester-year, of mundane teams enlivened by one or two groovy individuals. The disaster that was the home defeat to Bulgaria casts an immense shadow over French football – a second successive failure to qualify for the World Cup serves only to remind French footie how second-rate it has become once more. Amidst this gloom and despondency, Eric showed what a man he was by agreeing to take up the captaincy offered by coach Aime Jacquet – a poisoned chalice if ever there was one. Given that the French establishment saw fit to ban Eric for a year in '88 for accurately describing Henri Michel as a 'sac de merde', this surely shows how magnanimous our Eric is; he could easily have said "stuff it" and continued just to concentrate on his own game. Instead he stepped bravely forward but it seems that having feted his appointment, French observers will not let him lead in his own way.

Matters came to a head last month in Bratislava as the French opened their Euro'96 campaign against Slovakia. Eric had been brooding for months about the French press's negative, carping and personal criticisms of France's players; rightly he was also annoyed to be the one made to carry the can for others' failings. After all, the coach, not Eric, picks the team – and it is hardly Eric's fault that the rest of the team are not up to the standard of the class of '86. As Bernard Morlino (one of Eric's few journo friends and a contributor to "United We Stood") points out, the

French are ridiculous to compare Eric at United to Eric in France; "Here, some ask why Eric doesn't play as well for France. That's easily answered – compare the players! United are marvellously complementary whilst the French team is not. The players here just don't have that grace, Cantona excepted of course."

So it was hardly surprising, given this constant press barrage and Eric's essential dislike of hacks, that events in Slovakia took such an amusing turn. Firstly, Eric announced to the assembled journos that "if it was up to me, I'd piss on your collective arses" – nice one mon roi! Minutes later, he apparently turned on a hack from RTL who was asking impertinent questions and made several colourful threats before finally announcing to everyone that he was restricting their access to the team to "protect them from the media's malign influence". A smart, Fergusonesque move, you might think. Naturally, the more self-important and pompous of the French scribblers went apeshit. "L'Equipe", the most prestigious sports paper, lambasted every aspect of Eric's personality on and off the pitch under the headline "Have we got a captain on the team?" The article concluded "never for a moment did Cantona justify his new status as standard bearer for the Blues". Several papers slagged his performance in the 0-0 draw even though it was quite obvious to English viewers of Eurosport that Eric was the best player on the pitch. "France Football" magazine ran an editorial on the affair entitled "Who's afraid of Eric Cantona" claiming that the coach had lost control and was allowing Eric to run the show to the team's detriment. L'Equipe's Alain Constant summed up the view of the French press thus: "He's just not the right player to be captain. He is too much of an individual to be put in charge of a collective". Has this man seen Eric at United? Has he seen how, at his best, Eric makes the collective work by virtue of his own individual brilliance?

The press have also been getting at Eric on other running issues. David Ginola does not get on with Eric and they do not click on the pitch as yet; instead of blaming the over-rated and apparently unpleasant Ginola for this continued rift, they have instead decided it's Eric's fault. Similarly, Eric's successful personal campaign to have national games switched away from the Parc des Princes to provincial stadia – the Romania match took place at St. Etienne – has not found favour with hacks. Even though the atmosphere is much better away from the Parc and clearly therefore beneficial to the players, Paris based journos seem to be pissed off that they've got to trek out to the sticks to do their reports. I guess Eric would be quite happy if these pampered twats were to stay at home in their plush *seizième* apartments.

Even the president of the FFF, Claude Simonet, has felt compelled to add his pennyworth to the chorus of disapproval; "I'm unhappy about his attitude ... it's important that the team maintains good public relations". What a craven dickslurper he must be. Eric is a footballer, a leader and inspirer of players and a man of passionate honestly, not some bumlicking PR merchant. The French team is in disarray and Eric is their one great hope to lead them out of the morass. L'Equipe noted disapprovingly; "at the moment, Cantona seems to be the man in charge". The French have their heads too far up their arses to realise that it is far better to have a heroic figure like Eric at the helm than some lickspittle press groupie. As Eric said in his interview in United We Stood, "the French treat me like a capricious child". The French should beware: treat a kid like this and first he runs, then he leaves forever.

(Oct. 94)

The K-Standers, fresh from "Cantona – The Album" recording

MATCH REPORT: CRYSTAL PALACE AWAY, JAN. 25th 1995.

As I sat chain-smoking at half-time, a couple of mates turned up, having been delayed by court appearances and traffic snarl-ups. Panting breathlessly after sprinting across Thornton Heath, one asked if he'd missed anything. "Bugger all", I replied, "it's been the most tedious match of the season. You could've stayed at home and had no regrets." Four minutes later, football's equivalent of the A-bomb had exploded before us, threatening to devastate one man's career and his club's future. Picking up his dropped jaw from the floor, my neighbour murmured "I think you might've made a slight misjudgment there." Indeed – the most innocuous of mid-week tussles had, in a split-second, been transformed into the most infamous match of the decade.

Eric wasn't supposed to be the top-of-the-bill main bout, of course. This should have been Andy Cole's night, or so we hoped. The script was written in our minds – Cole scores, kickstarting a glorious OT striking career, thus leading United back to the table summit to round off an epic four days of Title assault. Selhurst Park, despite being a dustbin that can't decide whether it's a sporting complex, shopping village or rabbit warren, had until recently been a centre of Red Epiphany. The title-clincher in '93, the second championship party two weeks later and the Cup dream-performance last February had all been staged at this ugly suburban outpost. Sadly, it appears that the ground's lucky charm status really did turn sour for good last April. For Eric in particular, who had marked the beginning of his third year in English football with that celestial volley versus Wimbledon, Selhurst Park was about to cause the annulment of the Year Four commemorations.

The Red tribes, swelled by the habitual Cockney influx, annexed the entire left half of the Arthur Wait stand, which is truly a throwback to the ancien régime. A cavernous, vaguely Kippaxish old-timer, stuffed with decrepit wooden seats built for those with the backside of Kate Moss, smelling suspiciously of urine – luvverly. Much was later made of the allegedly aggressive, intimidating atmosphere generated by Palace but, bar one 'We support a local team' (who else would support Palace?), all I could hear were the Reds down the left flank. On an Endsleigh-bog pitch against an overtly physical bunch of local journeymen, we did little that I can now recall in the first-half. Somebody remarked upon the appalling lack of protection given to the leg-studded Cantona – *plus ça change* – but we thought nothing much of it at the time. All eyes darted nervously towards Cole whenever the ball approached him, Reds fighting furiously to prevent images of Gary Birtles settling in the mind, as we did our best vocally to keep the lad's spirits up. (You could groan *sotto voce* to yourself when he blundered but on no account was this to be expressed publicly.) Nil-nil at the break and the game was lucky to reach that.

The sole excitement in our stand had been provided by two ejections, carried out in the most mob-handed manner imaginable by the local sty's plod, as punishment for the most heinous crime of singing a song with a swear word in it. How remarkable that such a small-time, no-mark club should play host to the sort of hard-line crowd control tactics that would befit Belfast. As we soon discovered, Palace decline to impose such a policy throughout every stand.

And so to the moment of madness, the resurrection of Bruce Lee, the defining image of the season or whatever other label you like. Reds were still taking their post-lavatorial seats when a ball from our left looped limply over the heads of Eric and his marker/assassin Richard Shaw. Seconds earlier, Shaw had fouled Eric for the third time and gone unpunished once more. As the ball passed by, Eric extended a mildly petulant leg which, if it actually caught Shaw, could have done no more harm than a breath of summer breeze. Shaw appeared to hesitate, mid-air, for several seconds before apparently realising that the Oscar season was upon us. His gymnastic roll prompted Geordie Alan Wilkie to flash the most unwarranted red card Eric has ever received. Perhaps 'wor Alan' has a Toon shirt at home with 'Cole' on the back? Safe to say he won't be on Fergie's Christmas card list.

Our stand was imbued with resignation rather than shock. After all, it had been six months since Eric's last dismissal and our knowledge of English refs is such that we knew a red card was well overdue. We watched from a position directly opposite as Eric traipsed down the touchline with Norm 'Munster' Davies in half-hearted pursuit. If only he'd set off alongside him ...

Everyone I've spoken to since all had their eyes fixed on Eric. We saw what the TV cameras missed and what few cameras captured. Some lone lout, hardly the type that's supposed to be in a Family stand, hurtles several rows down to the front. His nastily naff leather-jacket is unmistakeable from even 70 yards – we are watching a creature from low down the food chain. He crosses 'the line' – not necessarily a physical mark on the ground but that boundary that we all recognize, the one that separates the players' universe from ours. He's in the 'no-man's-land' behind the hoardings, as close to the pitch as is possible without actually invading it, yet still a location in which a fan's presence would guarantee official intervention at any other ground. From our vantage point, he appears to be leaning over, inches from Cantona's face – he could be carrying a knife or bottle but a steward feet away does nothing. Someone shouts near me "what's he throwing?" (The better papers duly note that he appears to throw something, whether an object or a fist.) To us, it looks as though some sort of attempted assault is in preparation – but by the lout, not Eric. Norm chugs up at last, pulling Eric away and we think: 'it's all over' ... then something snaps within the mind of the genius and a hundred front pages are born. You've seen the rest.

It could have been so much worse – or better, depending on your point of view. For about five seconds as the pitch-side melée developed, a fan-player brawl seemed imminent. Despite the anchoring presence of the seats below us, you could feel a surging undercurrent throughout the Wait stand. Suddenly, we're in Red Army time warp: it's 1975 and we're about to stage an en masse pitch invasion. I look around and see that look in Red eyes all around, that manic gleam I'd almost forgotten and hear the time-honoured phrase "it's kickin' off." Had any other Palace-head attempted to lamp a Red shirted hero, the consequences could have been apocalyptic.

With hindsight, it's hard to credit but once Eric had been led off by a tea-drenched Schmeichel, Reds seemed to put all thoughts of the long-term consequences of Eric's action out of their minds. Instead, we focused completely on the struggle in hand – we were simply down to ten men and there were points to be won. Everything else could wait its turn. To say we were fired up would be an understatement – you could almost hear the adrenalin pumping through Red veins all around the stand. For fifteen minutes, we were at our best, a spell of passion both on and off the pitch that reminded you why you love United. Every man, woman and child in that stand remained on their feet throughout; every Red was, as requested, singing their hearts out for the lads. Driven forward by the greatest concerted awayday support for months, the improbable happened – just as my neighbour gasped "even May's got more chance of scoring than Cole", the Ginger One obliged with a header from Sharpe's cross. Needless to say, he put it straight into the keeper's arms with the goal at his mercy but it squirmed into the net nevertheless. 'Oo-ah Cantona', for the moment, was replaced by the first non-ironic 'Oo-ay, David May' of the season.

As we roared 'we've only got ten men' and 'you're so shit ...' the Reds pressed home the advantage. Sharpe hit the woodwork and Cole, through on goal at last, scooped it embarrassingly wide. Their scruffy, scrabbled, mud-drenched equalizer ten minutes from time took the edge off our righteous fervour momentarily but at the whistle, even though we were a man short, Reds were begging for more time to finish the job. It had been a performance built on passion and pride rather than skill and talent, but it deserved all three points.

For someone who's supposed to be a historian with a sense of the importance of events, it's a poor do to have to admit that I didn't really grasp the implications of Eric's actions until leaving the stand. Brooding on the lost points, pausing to watch the pack of Reds who hared down the hill to sort out a Palace mob, I was startled to hear a pair of Dwaynes discussing Eric's prospects using phrases such as 'life ban'. Only then, as police horses in the background clattered towards the warring fans yards away, did it strike me what the world would make of Eric's pugilistics. With battling Reds scarpering from the police in all directions, I reflected that the time for fighting had passed – somewhere out there under the London night-sky, the media would be preparing a gallows.

(First published in the author's book
"As The Reds Go Marching On ..." Aug. 95)

THE NEWEST TESTAMENT - THE TRIALS OF LE DIEU

THE TIES THAT BIND THE DEVOTED AND THEIR IDOL

Not the most inspirational headline ever to appear in 'The Independent' perhaps; however, only days after the kung-fu kick, the author grabbed the chance to defend our God in the national press as Reds began to rescue the agenda from those who sought to crucify Eric. Paddy led the way – we all followed, swords and pens aloft ...

Buried in the Sun's faxline column the day after the Selhurst Cantona Catastrophe was this glimpse into the secret heart of the Red hard-core: "Leave Eric alone. The supporter deserved it for wearing appalling clothes; Cantona should've hit him harder." Sarah from Hertfordshire, despite your sex and location, you are indeed 'one of us'.

'We', of course, are the thousands of Old Trafford zealots, the home-and-away brigade to whom Eric is known simply as 'Dieu'. Some of us are old enough to remember when Bruce Lee impressions and worse were a predictable feature of every terraced afternoon. 'We' were the shameless proles bellowing 'Oo-ah Cantona' for a solid ten minutes after the Frenchman's supposedly disgraceful exit last Wednesday. We are not, however, the alleged United fans whom the media hauled out of the Megastore on Thursday to parrot routine condemnations of the Blessed One. Nor are we much loved by Manchester United plc – or by anyone else for that matter. We are the Old Trafford Underclass: no-one likes us and we don't care, as Millwallians once sang.

What we like, however, is simple enough – thrills, passion and fight. All three values are encapsulated in and personified by the talismanic being of Eric Cantona. And if the rest of the world is allowed to continue worshipping their God, despite His two-footed challenges of earthquake, pestilence and famine, then we too can still smother Eric in adulation, forgiving his own temporary bouts of madness that hurt us all.

I must have spoken to nearly a hundred 'true Reds' over the past 48 hours; to a man, they stand squarely behind their King. Their sole desire is to see him back in the Red shirt – all other considerations remain secondary. To us, he is like the elder brother we look up to who's got into a 'spot of bovver with the law'; however much we disapprove of the offence, he is family and as such receives the automatic support that blood-ties engender.

Yes, we publicly accept the essential indefensibility of his actions but we will enter every possible plea of mitigation we can think of on his behalf to every debate, hearing or court to come; the defence campaigns have already begun. Some outsiders appear to find our refusal to cut

Cantona adrift astonishing or even disgusting but then how can an outsider comprehend the bonds that bind the devoted and their idol together? Remember that the greatest losers in this affair are the match-going United fans – our season is virtually destroyed, our icon's career on the edge of ruin and our dreams of the European Holy Grail banished. Yet still we love him. Woe betide any who would seek to divorce the lovers from the loved; ten thousand enraged Reds waving broken bottles outside your front door is not a prospect to be welcomed, I would have thought.

Above all, spare us the sanctimonious waffle paid by the yard that is spouted by the monstrous legion of ex-pros and soi-disant experts. Eric has not traumatized millions of children or brought the game to the brink of the precipice. Football needs the Cantonas as much as the Linekers – the Establishment might not admit it but this is an entertainment industry that thrives as much on horrendous controversy and appalling ill-deeds as it does on good play and clean living. Brawls, bungs, drugs and karate – we love 'em all. Save your 'family values' for the tennis club: "Keep Football Filthy" is our slogan for the post-PC Nineties.

(First published in 'The Independent' Jan. 95)

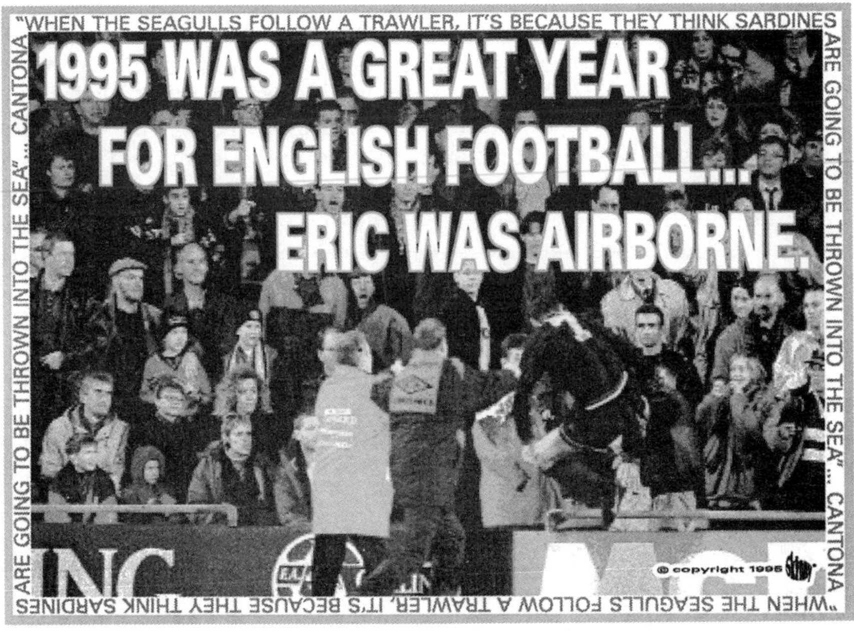

THE KIDS ARE ALRIGHT

I'll be honest with you. Like many Reds I spoke to during the Selhurst Shellshock aftermath, I couldn't give a toss about such concerns as 'setting a bad example to children' or 'bringing disrepute to the game'. Whenever I hear sanctimonious waffle on such subjects, I do as Goebbels and reach for the revolver. Disrepute is the lifeblood of the soap opera that is British football. Imagine a Premiership peopled by those of the purest Lineker mentality; the game would be dead in three years, bored to tears by relentless godliness. As for the kiddies, I would suggest that football already kow-tows to family values quite enough as it is, thank you; besides, any parent who either a) seeks to make a bleedin' footballer their child's role model or b) seeks to shield the little chap from all life's nasties, hardly deserves much sympathy.

However, if we must pretend to be sensible, serious and – ugh – responsible, then we can still find cause to say 'bollox' to the sanctimony-peddlars. Just what example did Eric set, after all? Surely it was an object lesson in what can befall the miscreant? Misbehave on the field and look what happens to you, kiddies – crucifixion and a six-month ban. From the 'bad example', you can teach the 'good lesson', as every pedagogue knows. On 'Granada Upfront', some lynch mob lemming reckoned that kids all over the country would now be attempting to execute Bruce Lee dropkicks on innocent spectators. Even if such a moronic prophesy were to come true, what of it? If every footballer were held responsible for the imitative actions of every brain-dead teenager in the land, what absurdities would result? Here's a story from '90 Minutes': 14-year old Graham Evans tried to copy Jurgen Klinsmann's diving celebration but got stuck in the mud doing so, breaking his ankle. Hugely amusing, of course, doubly so for him being Scottish, but should Klinsmann be hauled before an FA tribunal for setting such a potentially dangerous example to kids? Or be 'held responsible' for the negligent antics of a stranger? Get real!

Having mentioned the Tottenham Teuton, it reminds me of a perfect illustration of what truly constitutes 'bringing the game into disrepute.' I once met a relative of the Milan defender Costacurta on an Adriatic beach. As is natural between two male strangers, football became the main topic of conversation within 60 seconds and he proceeded to tell me how devastated the player had been to miss the European Cup Final. Not only would history record him as missing from the honour role of the greatest club display of this generation but also he had suffered unbearable torments during the semifinal, when he feared that his sending off was going to cost his mates and their legions of fans the Final place they'd spent two years trying to achieve.

Now remember who put him in that position – Jurgen Klinsmann. It was his wanton, deliberate impression of an assassinated President when there had in fact, been no contact whatsoever that set off that catastrophic chain of events for the young Italian. Fortunately, Monaco still lost the game but Klinsmann emerged unscathed and unpunished, able to ply his trade for the loathsome, cynical German team in USA '94 and then at that temple of cheating disgrace, White Hart Lane. As I write this, Klinsmann is on 'Sportsnight', being lionized by an orgasmic Motson and subtly portrayed as a 'decent foreigner' in contrast to the 'despicable' Cantona. Vomit-inducing is too mild an epithet. If you're looking for 'bad examples' to children, if you're seeking events that 'bring the game into disrepute', if you're looking for genuinely dastardly foreign villains, then I suggest to you that Eric would have to have sliced someone's testicles off to come anywhere near the crime perpetrated by Klinsmann that night. The 'victim' at Selhurst Park was a repulsive creature who had brought the assault upon himself and who deserved, and received, no sympathy at all. The Klinsmann victim was just a decent player, robbed of his just rewards. Now Cantona is banned and disgraced – Klinsmann has become the 'good German' loved by all. Pass the bucket.

(First published in 'Zeitgeist', Feb. 95)

LEARNING LESSONS AT THE COURT OF KING ERIC

It was supposed to be an enjoyable enough wheeze; fifteen of us down in London to appear with Boylie on 'The Big Breakfast', promoting 'Eric The King', headed off to Croydon Magistrates' Court for an Eric-supporting singsong. After all, it was going to be a formality, right? The only debate would be how big a fine Eric would get; no harm in us entertaining the media-hounds while the world waited for a decision. Ha. By mid-day, we were left reflecting not on a successful day's record-PR but on our witnessing first hand one of the most shocking episodes of this increasingly seismic season.

Turning the corner onto the court road just after ten, we marvelled at the sight outside the entrance, a camera-rich sprawl of over 400 hacks, technicians and curious onlookers but with scarcely a Red to be seen. The media vultures were spread across the pavement, along the central reservation and on top of every available roof – as we legged across the road, roaring 'Eric the King', every telephoto lens and video camera swung towards us, capturing Boylie's Boys and the K-Stand placards in their full glory. As we dished out press releases and gave interviews, convincing the most sceptical of hacks that all Reds are behind Eric, we gleaned that the media were mostly bored. They didn't expect much of a real news story to emerge here, just an anti-climactic fine; this was merely a circus of visual images, capturing pix of media scrums and harassed celebs. The guys with the notebooks assumed they'd be in for an underworked afternoon and had nothing better to do than talk to the likes of us, busy reciting lyrics and badmouthing Simmons. They were, at least, grateful that Eric had typically eschewed the limo and walked the three minutes from hotel to court, seemingly none the worse for his night of champagne, clubbing and gig by the Artist Formerly Known As Talented. At least that guaranteed them the 'celeb surrounded by press pack' pictures that papers rather tediously demand these days.

So there we all stood for the best part of two hours, the world's eyes and ears patiently waiting for news from the lucky recipients of Press Pool passes inside. As we sweated gently under the London sun, Pete Boyle clambered up some vacant ladders to lead us through a few terrace classics to the bemusement of assembled hackery; a few shy London Reds turned up to swell our numbers, whilst the half-dozen Palace fans knocking around kept very, very quiet indeed. The Anti-Nazi League, there to make the most of the anti-racist opportunity, pointed these creatures out to us: 'South London Scum', said one succinctly. Later, with us Reds long gone, these vermin suddenly found their tongues when Eric finally emerged: typical standards of Palace bravery, making a stand only when there's no chance of a come-back. No doubt Simmons had thought himself similarly secure when he stepped forward that fateful night ...

Getting inside to see how the King was doing – Incey's committal being an early formality – was harder than getting a face-value away ticket. Southy successfully found a way of making repeated ten minute trips to the court bogs without being promptly ejected, thus being able to emerge to tell us how cool Eric was looking, mixing his customary swagger with some required elements of humble penitence. Amidst the steady stream of exiting local crims, bemoaning their latest drug-dealing fines on mobile phones, came Red-friendly journos whom we corralled behind our pen to pump for info. Jim White of the Indie seemed cautiously happy: "poor prosecution performance" and "Eric's behaving himself" gave us heart. Then the BBC North correspondent, attracted by our chorus of "one Charlie Lambert", told us about the reading of Simmons's uncensored statement and that two of the bench were women. By 11.30, any lingering worries we'd had were dispelled. Eric's brief had been excellent whereas theirs had been lack-lustre; Eric had said all the right things and pushed all the right emotional buttons; a female-dominated bench, knowing what your typical prim, twinset mag.-woman is like, would surely be in thrall to Eric's brooding charm and appalled by Simmons's language. The verdict would be at any moment, then down the pub with the hacks for some Boylie buffoonery on table-tops with lager-tops.

But the bench weren't straight back at all. As the delay stretched on past twenty minutes and hacks jostled impatiently for shot-positions, my own alcohol-pangs were replaced by well-founded concern. What could be taking so long to discuss? I turned to a K-Stander and remarked that they must be debating more than the mere size of a fine; this was sounding like one mag. arguing for a fine, one undecided and one pressing for something much worse. Having once been in Eric's position myself, I knew the warning signs only too well.

Even so, when the news broke, the 'thrill' of being there at the epicentre of a newsquake (c. Chris Morris) was memorable only for the sense of horrified shock. Southy and Peter Peet ran out, white-faced, to tell us the worst; for a moment, we guffawed at their attempted kidology, only for the sentence to be confirmed by the racing hacks behind them. Journalists are not, by their nature, easily taken aback, but today those correspondents around us were genuinely appalled. For about three minutes, chaos reigned as journos tried to piece together the facts before animated debates about legal processes broke out everywhere. Was Eric going straight down? Could you actually get time for common assault as a first-time offender? Could you appeal against a sentence like that? "What the f*ck happens now?" screamed a quality journo, "someone please tell me, now! " For about 60 seconds my head was in pieces, like the rest of the lads; I recovered sufficiently to dredge up old criminal process lessons and tell the hack that, whatever happened, a judge-in-chambers had to be found immediately to give Eric bail pending appeal. (Such is British justice – our magistrates cannot be allowed to operate unless tended by a fireman-judge, ready to rush in to correct patent miscarriages like this.) Thankfully, Maurice Watkins did find one, down the road at the Crown Court, who did the necessary: we, of course, wouldn't have left the scene unless we'd known Eric's freedom was secured.

Suddenly, the massed media snapped back into gear, looking for someone, anyone, who would go on the record to provide confirmation of what the journos clearly felt – that a judicial outrage had just been perpetrated. With evident relief, they remembered they had some genuine Reds from Manchester on hand; the pack descended on us, pulling us all over the pavement to speak to camera, mike and dictaphone. Lads who'd never spoken to the media in their life ended up doing half-a-dozen interviews, to the nationals, radio and TV; how surreal to see Southy, the most down-to-earth, unmetropolitan lad imaginable, going straight from 'The Times' to French TV's main news crew ...

Our duty done, we withdrew from the battleground, staying just long enough to salute The Guvnor when he finally emerged. Some of us had been up for 36 hours already and Mancunian beds were calling. On the journey home, we listened dumbfounded as the media explosion ran its course on every radio station in Christendom, several bulletins opening with comments by Pete and the boys, intermingled with us singing 'Eric the King' outside the court. Some of us realised that for once, we – not the media or superstore part-timers – had set the agenda. This wasn't like the original kung-fu aftermath, when true Reds had to struggle to rescue the news agenda after sad twats had condemned our King on air, whilst we were all still stuck on coaches returning from Selhurst. We had got on first, and spoken in the most cutting, condemnatory way possible about the crass misjudgment – in doing so, that challenged any naysayers to go against the prevailing orthodoxy, always a difficult task on a running news story once the initial die is cast. Besides, once BBC Radio stations had broadcast us saying that 'the magistrates deserve a good karate-kicking', anyone else going on to defend Eric would sound quite moderate and reasonable in comparison ...

Now this is sounding a bit self-congratulatory, which was not the intention. It may well be that our presence and contributions made no difference, that the press and media would have taken just such a pro-Eric line in any event, purely on the case's merits. Maybe so, but who can be sure? Apart from writing this to let those who couldn't be there know what it was like, there is a point to this. It has been argued in the past that Reds should not discuss anything with the media, that we will be 'used' by journos who are scumbags anyway and that those who engage in these activities run the risk of being seen as self-promoting media-groupies. That day at Eric's court has convinced me that this argument, though appealing, is nevertheless to be rejected. Two particular remarks that day lead me to conclude that Reds should take every opportunity offered to air their views publicly (as long as they are pro-'true' United, of course.) A very famous journo remarked to me that the world divides into two: agenda-setters and agenda-followers. Power, of course, lies with the former. "Get in early, seize the initiative and repeat what you're saying to everyone at every opportunity," he advised "and you'll find the media and the authorities will follow." Later, a radio analysis featured a summary of the day's 'expert comments'; the presenter noted that all the legal-eagles had talked of the media influence on the magistrates and that the relentlessly anti-Eric nature of much of it must have convinced the court that the public would allow them to 'get away with' imposing such a draconian sentence.

So, at the risk of being branded a media-slag, let me put this to you. Our justice system – and all quasi-legal authorities like the FA etc. – do not, as they are supposed to do, operate independently of mob opinion. In fact, in a mass-media dominated age, 'authority' increasingly kowtows cravenly to public opinion as selected, distorted and presented by the media and by, in particular, the press. Forget rules of evidence, codes of punishment and the like; authorities of any kind now act on the basis of what the lynch mob, as represented by the tabloid, will allow. If you want to make the world's powers treat United, our players and us in the best, most favourable fashion possible, you have one target you can influence – the media.

And because they have, essentially, an open agenda, you can make a difference. Control the media and you control the world. Party politics apart, papers have no fixed principles of any sort. They will go with whatever sells, with whatever will 'run' and with whatever doesn't offend its core readership or advertisers. The consumer is king and that man is you. What is more, MUFC supporters have a potential power to influence the media, and therefore the powers that create our football-supporting conditions, that no-one else can rival. Not only is our Club the most newsworthy in itself anyway, but we are also the most numerous consumers by a mile compared to any other Club. We didn't get our act together in the past, or did so too late or too half-heartedly; whilst we were discussing who we'd allow to talk to us about Eric, the media and the authorities were already way ahead of us, building a gallows. We have so much power but never use it – do you think The Sun's trio of cretinous football writers would still be allowed to maintain their anti-United, anti-Eric vendettas if we'd boycotted the bastard paper? Look what Liverpool fans achieved with their boycott – turned The Sun pro-Liverpool within the year. We have treble Pool's fans, so what could we achieve? Anything, mate. I'll put it crudely: the media follows what they think the public wants; the authorities, in turn, follow the media. If you did absolutely nothing to protest against Eric's treatment, beyond arguing about him in the pub with Bluenoses, then you haven't really been much of a help have you? The media – and therefore the authorities – will follow the lead given by whoever makes the most noise. So write angry letters, get onto phone-ins, use faxlines, hassle TV programmes and generally get yourself involved with the media whenever there is a cause to be fought because otherwise your power as a Red is lost to us. And if you get the chance to put the true Red view on radio or on TV, do it. It may well be purer, ideologically sounder and cooler to say 'f*ck off' but it doesn't help build a more Red-friendly world.

(From the author's book, "As The Reds Go Marching On",
first extracted in 'Red Issue' April 95)

THE DAILY SPURT **March 24th 1995**

STRING 'ER UP!

Outrage at bonkers beak

The magistrate who sentenced Eric Cantona to two weeks pokey, Mrs Jean Pearch, is at the centre of a tabloid storm, with her sentence being replayed time and time again by a slavering media.

PUNISHMENT

"What sort of example is she setting the children?" asked one despairing onlooker. "I try to teach my kids to respect the law and authority but when they see her going over-the-top like that, they just won't listen to me."

"She's in big trouble now" warned one legal-eagle. "When a judge gets hold of that sentence, he's going to come down on her like a ton of bricks. I wouldn't be surprised if she got suspended from the Croydon Mags First Team for a start."

UNDERSTANDABLE

But there were some there to defend her. A Miss Patricia Crerand, respected ex-magistrate, said she could understand Pearch's actions. "You know what it's like up there, with all those people having a go at you, with all the media attention and the pressure to perform; sometimes you get a rush of blood, you over-react and then, bang, you've gone in two-footed with a two-weeker. It could happen to anyone."

INEVITABLE

Mrs. Pearch already had a reputation as a hard-line disciplinarian, promising to the Croydon Advertiser that she'd be cracking down on offenders; many predicted that with her track record of going in hard, something like this was inevitable. The Sun have claimed that it's all part of her genetic make-up – "a Christian mother from Norbury, what do you expect?" – but whatever the reason for her moment of madness, she would now be ill-advised to go anywhere near Manchester.

TRAUMA

Meanwhile, the after-effects are plain to see. "My kid was terrified when he heard that sentence" said one father; "it could have traumatized him for life, hearing that." And in Manchester schoolyards, the hot new game is called 'Croydon Magistrates', with eight-year-olds being sentenced to Chinese burns or beatings for late five-a-side tackles. Mrs. Pearch was unavailable for comment and is also an old bag.

(Apr. 95)

'DEAR ERIC ...'

As if Eric's ban wasn't burden enough to carry, our shoulders began creaking even more ominously when Inter Milan turned up, waving billion-lira contracts in Eric's face. We prepared for the worst and made our desperate last appeals, the author getting a front-page chance to plead directly to God with an open 'Dear Eric' letter in 'The Independent'. Months later, Fergie himself was still quoting lines from this piece and praised it in his book thus: "Fabulous – it was a great article". Thanks, Boss.

"Notre cher Eric,

Rumour has it that the Milanese piranhas have sensed your blood is in the water after that nasty Pearch attack and are coming in to snap you up. As another semi-hinged magician once said, you cannot be serious. Inter Milan of 'tangentopoli'? Didn't you have your fill of gangsters at Marseilles? Martin Edwards may be sharp but at least his violin case contains a musical instrument, if you get my drift. Let me appeal to your Bonapartist sense of honour and tradition. Could you really exchange the Red of United, the symbol of glory, flair and self-expression, for the dull stripes of Inter, the club who gave us catenaccio, Euro Cup bungs and a succession of psychotic international full-backs? And what of your burning ambition, to be crowned the King of the European Champions? Inter are the Manchester City of Italian football: they will never become the best team in their city, let alone country or continent. As a good existentialist, you have no truck with facile notions of 'destiny' but you have spoken of your mission to lead us back to the Elysian fields on which we last gambolled in '68. Abandon this admittedly Herculean, mould-breaking task now and you will forever regret it: you will have become the David Owen of football. Stick with us and prepare for government.

Are you still not convinced? Then be threatened by brutal honesty. You are one of the great egoists of the age, on a par with Jim Morrison and Mick Jagger, radiating the arrogance of one who has much about which to be arrogant. You hog centre-stage and hug the limelight, revelling in your supremacy over the mere mortals of opposition. How will such a Lion King fare in Italy's Serie A, though? Clogging, donkey centre-halves are in short supply there, mon roi, where you will discover the number five and six shirts conceal the lithe torsos of deadly assassins. The space and freedom you exploit here will be replaced by confinement and the oppression of man-marking. Serie A's Clubs are stuffed full of luminous talents, players who are the best their countries have produced: no longer will you be the only pole star in the constellation. Forget the individualist liberty you exalt at Old Trafford – in Italy, the collective is all. You will be forced to conform or join the rest of the libero-spirited, languishing in Serie A Reserves. Besides, the Italians cannot stand to be out-poseured, especially not by the French. You are a challenge to their preening sense of virility, un vrai homme amidst a nation of mamma's boys. Just ask Dennis Berkgamp.

Above all, in true Geminian fashion, you need to be loved. Could anyone adore you like we do? You're not even on the pitch yet we sing for you like we do for no other. We wear you name with pride wherever we go, we champion your cause at every opportunity, we bow to your picture that has replaced the Pope's by our bedside every night. You have become more than a mere star or hero or leader: in crowning you the King of Old Trafford, the first to reign since Law, you have become an icon of religious scale. The Number 7 shirts we wear bear the simple legend 'Dieu'. How much more homo-erotic can you expect us manly Mancs to be in order to persuade you of our eternal fidelity? You once called United 'your perfect wife' – what grounds have we given you for divorce? As Macmillan would say, 'these little local difficulties' will soon pass and the forty weeks in the wilderness will be over. Return to the bosom of your forgiving family at O.T. and let us bellow 'Eric The King' for you once more.

(First published in 'The Independent' Mar. 95)

THE KING IS NOT DEAD - LONG LIVE THE KING!

Thursday April 27th 1995: a date to be burned into every Red cerebral cortex forever. Exactly three months before, every media outlet in the land had been filled with 'that' picture, the portrayal of the act whose consequences threatened to remove the King from his Old Trafford throne for good. Jesus spent forty days in the wilderness: 'Dieu' has had to suffer more than twice as long. But as Thursday's Evening News hit the mid-day streets, Reds all over town rejoiced at the sight of the banner headline: 'ERIC WILL STAY WITH THE REDS'. As glorious restorations of monarchs go, this beat even Charles the Second's. And as once the Cavaliers stuck two fingers up at the Puritans, so Reds have delighted in our triumph over the rest of Britain, as represented by the media scum-bags. They tried their best to force him out and failed: one-nil to the Champions.

How sweet the spectacular misjudgments of, for example, that week's Daily Mirror. On Tuesday, they'd announced as fact that Eric was going – even better, that very Thursday morning, the Mirror's Nigel Clarke had spent two pages detailing all the reasons why Eric had decided to leave. Truly, the 'Mirror' has reached 'Sun' levels of bullshit over-production. The egg smeared over their fat faces will take some getting off, won't it?

A mention too for Patrick Barclay, so-called Sportswriter of the Year of the 'Observer' and a regular on the Red-baiting 'Hold the Back Page', who has come to epitomize all those hacks who hate United's fans as well as players. Only a week before, he filled eight columns denouncing United supporters, telling us how disgraceful it was that we should still be singing for Eric at every game, laughing at our 'naive' belief that such support would encourage Eric to stay. So much for his award-winning judgment, then, when Eric made it clear that it was precisely this continued, devoted support that played a huge part in persuading him to stay. To those who risked the ridicule from the cynical by singing 'Eric the King' etc. at every game since Selhurst Park, take a bow. For once, we were heard.

To all our rivals who've been wetting themselves with excitement at the prospect of Eric leaving, tough break lads. It seems the 'where's yer Cantona' songs will have to be shelved for a while yet. To City fans in particular, special commiserations. We fully understand how your arses must be collapsing at the thought of more Eric-inspired derby slayings.

In fact, the list of those whose faces we now want to laugh in, spit at and stamp on is endless. The Cantona Affair has polarized the 'us and them' situation like nothing else in living memory. These past three months have brought all true Reds closer together, huddled around our Club and our King: with a few noble exceptions, everyone outside Old Trafford's Red-blooded family has become the enemy. So a simple 'f*ck off, world' will suffice. No-one likes us and we don't care 'cos we've got our King back.

Let us also recognize a rare event – the Club has showed the strength, pride and courage to dismiss the easy option. Not only have they resisted a multi-million fee – bet the shareholders loved that – and put a half-decent offer on the table but they have stood up for an important principle. It was argued everywhere that Eric had to leave because the tension surrounding his eventual playing return would be unbearable for him, the team and the Club. The media made it clear that they would do their best to hype that tension up even further.

The message was that they, the authorities and opposing fans would, in unholy alliance, threaten to make Eric's life hell unless United bowed to their demands to expel Eric from England. This was made explicit by the National Federation of Football Supporters' Clubs, who let the cat out of the bag with their statement in Cup semi week. Credit United, then, that instead of opting for the easy life, they refused to cave in to mob rule. It is, after all, the same principle that all parrot in relation to football hooliganism: we must play on, not allow the thugs to win. What sort of morality would sanction the hounding from England of a great player, simply because he was too unpopular amongst football's observers? Where would it end? Who would be next for the lynch-mob treatment? There are too many amidst the 'football establishment' who appear to have taken their civics lessons from the Ku Klux Klan.

Above all, let us appreciate the bravery of the hero of the hour, of the year, of the decade. He could have doubled his money; he could have made a fresh start; he could have escaped a country which has imprisoned and demonized him; he could have revelled in a great, new challenge in the world's greatest league; he could have enjoyed the fervent worship of a whole new city and country. Instead, he has chosen to stay, at a Club who won't be in the European Cup this season, who still don't pay him properly and who are hated beyond all others. This from a man whose main goal is to be a Euro Champ, who sees a salary level only as an indication of how much a Club really values him and who has often expressed a need to be loved and appreciated by all who see him, not just his Club's fans. Against all the odds, he really has, as the song has it, declared "this Club's his perfect wife". What a man.

(May 95)

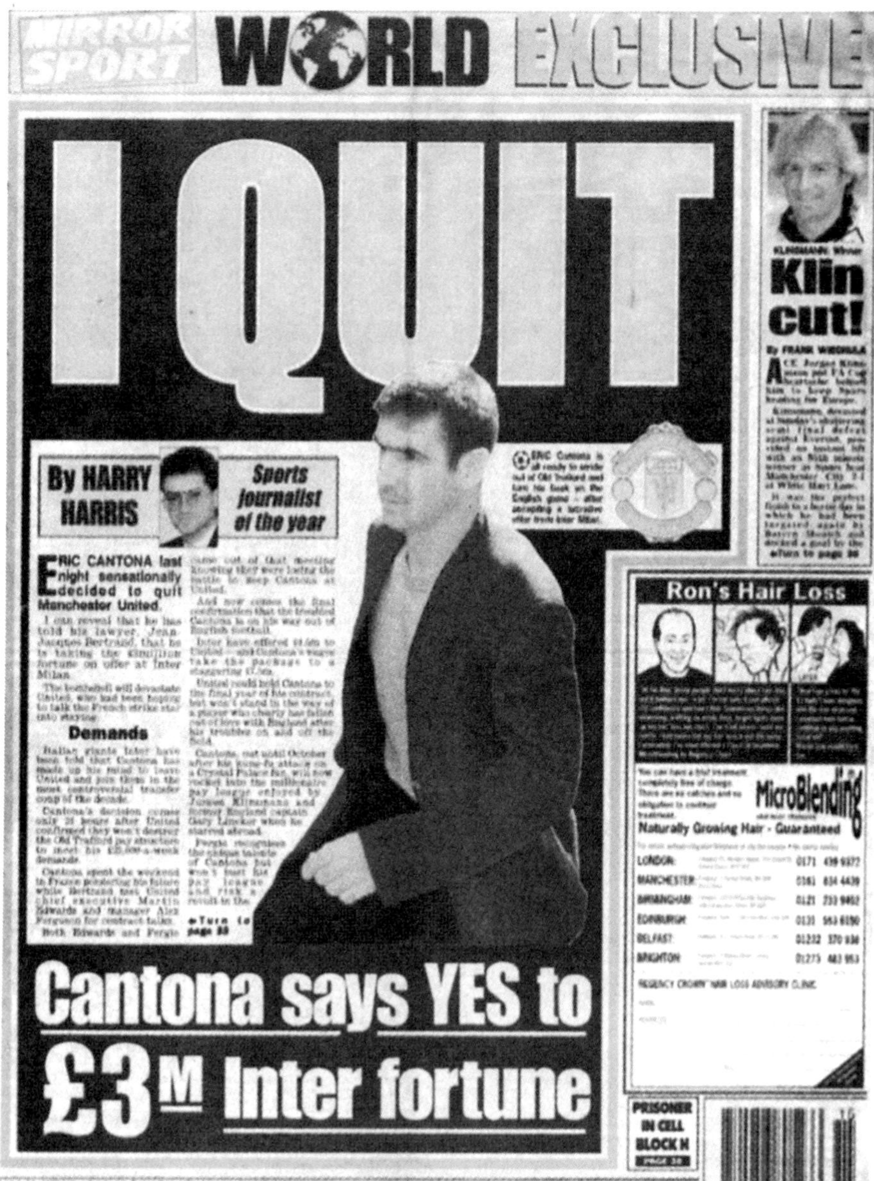

MIRROR SPORT

WORLD EXCLUSIVE

I QUIT

By HARRY HARRIS

Sports journalist of the year

ERIC CANTONA last night sensationally decided to quit Manchester United.

Demands

Klin cut!

Ron's Hair Loss

MicroBlending

Naturally Growing Hair - Guaranteed

PRISONER IN CELL BLOCK H

Cantona says YES to £3M Inter fortune

Another Harry Harris triumph . . .

SHARP
UMBRO
UMBRO
©LOZ'95

DEIFYING A DEVIL

Biblical students will recall that Lucifer was once an angel sitting at God's side before he got relegated to the Endsleigh League (Hell Division). Eric has travelled the other way: vilified by the world as Satan's spawn, the ultimate Red-mist Devil, in January 95, Old Trafford's faithful worshippers have since first canonized and now, finally, deified him. 'FourFourTwo' asked the author to attempt an explanation.

"For Man United fans, the close-season took off where the campaign proper ended – applying thumping one-twos to the solar plexus. Hard on the heels of the Double Defeat came the knock-down sell-offs: the Guvnor and the Legend exited stage-left from the pantheon of heroes. But then, there are heroes and there are heroes, differing degrees of divinity on a Hinduesque basis. For however shattering these two losses were, at least 'Dieu' remained. As one hard-core Red put it: "I'm angry about Ince; I'm sad about Hughes. But if they let Eric go, I'd be lookin' at a double manslaughter charge." Messrs Ferguson and Edwards, I think he was only half-joking.

Since the Selhurst Park debacle, Eric has often been referred to as a 'cult hero' which gives the misleading impression that Cantona-worship is an obsession for a minority. If you've attended any United match this season, however, you'll have learned the truth. At the risk of 'Four-FourTwo' ending up on bonfires in the Philippines and Deep South, Eric is currently more frenziedly adored in the Red three-quarters of Manchester than Jesus, Take That and Ryan Giggs combined. This is no cult: it's mass devotion that drenches thousands in the juices of love.

The media has a propensity to calculate anything Red-centred in terms of merchandise and money so let us measure it thus. Tour the barrows of the Old Trafford market-place and you will currently find twenty-three varieties of Cantona T-shirt. The 'Eric The King' video is the best-selling player-vid ever. There are more Club shirts with 'Cantona', 'Dieu' or, er, 'Le God' stamped on the back than all the rest of the team combined. His autobiography took up residency in the Top Ten lists and even sold well when it was only available on French-language import. The indie record label Exotica released the song 'Eric The King' as a low-key single and were astonished to see it shoot into the indie top ten en route to becoming the best-selling indie footie record ever: a Cantona album is due in October. If you're soul-less enough to see these things in purely bottom-line terms, the man's pre-eminence is fiscally unchallenged.

For the lads on what were once the terraces, the devotion is more simply expressed – in song. During his long, painful absence when the consequences of his kung-fu conspired to cost us our Double, did we hold it against him or just allow him to slip from our thoughts? Of course not: with perhaps typical Mancunian perversity, our sessions of vocal hosannas doubled and trebled in frequency and intensity. Not a match was allowed to pass without our reminding both Eric and the world of our chosen religion: the Cantona Medley became the mainstay of the K-Stand Song-book. At the last count, there were eight fully-fledged Cantona songs, all of which you are likely to hear renditioned in any particular game. And whilst it may be true that the high priest of Ericism, Peter Boyle, originates most of them, they are taken up by thousands within moments. How gratifying, then, that in the face of media criticism of our 'shameless' behaviour, Eric should have cited our efforts to support him as a prime reason for re-signing. For Rob Shepherd, Patrick Barclay etc. it may seem an 'obscene obsession' but as any Red of the political kind would remind you, the ends justify the means. Eric will be back with a vengeance and that is all that matters.

If, as Basil Fawlty said to Sybil, your specialized subject is the bleedin' obvious, you might explain this Gallophilic frenzy with a simple reference to his footballing ability: he is the best player at the Club ergo he is the most adored. That, however, would be as howlingly simplistic as crediting the Beatles phenomenon to their unusual chorus chord-shifts. Nor is it enough merely to add that his pivotal role in ending our 26-year Title-free starvation was enough to elevate him to the heavens, important an aspect though that is. It may be true that for Red intellectuals, the star quality baggage that comes with Cantona – the philosophy, the painting, the style – adds hugely to his appeal, making him truly admirable in a way that your average monosyllabic, 'Loaded'-reading provincial trundler can never be, however good a player. But for Reds, particularly of my post-60s generation, there is something more elemental to it than all that.

Firstly, those of us who were too young for 1968 and the Holy Trinity of Best, Law and Charlton have something to cherish that inhabits the same plane as those 60s legends, something about which we can rhapsodize to our kids, an era to mythologize for evermore. At last we have been there in person to witness a team that could give the Sixties side a match – and, in doing the Double and retaining the Title, a team that in some ways has outstripped their illustrious forebears. Cantona was the jewel of that team, a veritable Koh-inoor and the catalyst of the success: moreover, we have at last our own contemporary hero fit to be mentioned in the same breath as Best & Co. However much we loved Robson, Hughes, Whiteside and Hill, none ever quite reached that pinnacle. But Eric, surely, has done so.

Secondly, Eric has become more than mere flesh, even more than a holy talisman. He has, especially since Selhurst Park, become the personification of United. It isn't just that our own siege mentality has produced an empathy with his own personal beleaguerment; it's because in Eric, we see a distillation of everything that we like to think we are. We see style as important as function; we exalt the individual over the collective; we rejoice in the very qualities the English are supposed to disdain – glamour, sexiness, arrogance, and hot-tempered exhibitionism. Not for us the moralising, humble and dogged Protestant work ethic of the rest. We always reckoned United were not quite of this world: now, both Eric and us are United as spiritual Continentals stuck in a downbeat English league. Vive la difference – and vive l'entente cordiale!

(First published in 'FourFourTwo', Aug. 1995)

Dog & Partridge Reds receive news of Alan Ball's appointment

RED OCTOBER

October the first, 1995, to be precise: two suspensions, a court sentence, a media lynching and one rather alarming Parisian walkabout later, the King returned to his supplicant minions. It seems hardly co-incidental that the duration of his sojourn was approximately that of a pregnancy. No birth has been so anxiously, frenziedly awaited; 34,000 expectant parents looked on, hoping he'd emerge from the womb-like Old Trafford tunnel as beautiful as they'd dreamed he'd be. And like every parent who prays the kid'll be alright, all limbs and senses in perfect order, our exhilaration at witnessing the rebirth, the Second Coming, was surely tempered by similar worries. Would his touch be as good, his vision unimpaired, his genius undimmed? The pompous media-crats decreed that Cantona 'owed' us, that he had a debt to repay to the faithful: thank you then, Eric, for taking only 67 seconds to dispel our every concern.

That Eric's own particular contributions – making the opener and scoring the match-saver – were ridiculously, cinematically dramatic shouldn't have surprised and astonished us as much as it did. It was, after all, quintessential Cantona. To reword Sherlock Holmes: with Eric, you must remove everything that is predictable or normal – whatever is left, however incredible or seemingly impossible, is what Eric will do.

The rest of the day's carnival was, in contrast to Cantona's effervescent quantum physics, Newtonianly predictable: the tricolour-drenched crowd was good though never 70s-great, the media multiple-orgasmed themselves dry, Pete Boyle got extra-strengthedly pissed, Lee Sharpe was f*cking hopeless. All played their supporting roles tight to the scripted word, leaving Eric to ad-lib and free-form at will. Liverpool, too, played their usual part of recent times, outclassing and outpassing us for 60 minutes, superior in almost every key position but Eric's. If you could detach yourself sufficiently from the emotional maelstrom that Eric's return engendered, you'd have written-off United for the season on this performance, our first match of 95/6 against a truly good side. But who could detach oneself from the cosmically magnetic Cantona Force? However much Liverpool exposed our loss of Ince, Hughes and Andrei, the moribundity of Bruce, our overdose of youthful callow and our lack of tactical and teamplay cohesion, as long as Eric remains, so does the dream – the dream that he can lead those around him to maturity and dominance.

To be realistic, we all know we can count on nothing. The sheer mercuriality that makes him so brilliant also makes him unchainable. By the time you read this, he may already have left. He may go next summer, winter or spring: he may die happy here at the age of 120, having devoted his life to us. Who knows? But remember Eric's existentialism: he, surely, would tell us to forget the past – it cannot control us – and to dismiss notions of destiny or eternal commitment. All that matters is here and now, how we define ourselves every day through our present actions. When a loved family member almost dies, you appreciate and enjoy his presence so much more intensely afterwards – you've come face to face with what you could have lost. However long Eric stays at our side, live each day as if it could be the last, to the max. Whether this is his swan song, his Indian Summer or just the start of the brightest supernova of his career, envelop yourself in it. Go to every Eric game, sing every song, join every hosanna – because we'll never see his like again. As they cried in 1789, vive la revolution Française!

(Oct. 1995)

Part Two:

THE GOOD, THE BAD AND THE DODGY

1. 'Eight And A Half' – Starring Alex Ferguson
2. Fergie's Tactical Masterclass
3. The Lone Gunman At The O.T. Corral
4. "Ee-Ay, Paddio"
5. "Ooh-Ay, David May"
6. Play The May Way
7. So That The Meek Shan't Inherit The Earth
8. United We Should Stand

"EIGHT AND A HALF" - STARRING ALEX FERGUSON

... in which the author attempts to condense the plot of 'United We Stood' into 2,500 words for the benefit of 'FourFourTwo' readers wanting a retrospective on the Fergie Years. The author sent Alex a copy of this as a peace offering after their summer spat but fears it may not have been 'arslikan' enough for the Boss. You be the judge ...

As noted film buff and Fergie favourite son Choccy McClair could doubtless remind you, Fellini's "8½" told the dramatically intense and often surreal story of a director's struggle against the odds to complete his life's masterpiece. And happily for this strained allusion, Alex Ferguson's doom-laden Wembley appearance in May marked eight and a half seasons of his own directorial tenure at the Theatre of Dreams, a time stuffed with enough plot-twists and climaxes to keep any movie-goer satisfied. Neatly, Alex has ended his eighth full season as he ended his first – in second place behind Kenny Dalglish, natch – but with his star billing so enhanced as to be second only to Sir Matt Busby's. His life's masterpiece may yet be rewarded with a European Cup but for now let us reflect on how he has become, in Cantona's phrase, the much-worshipped 'head of our family' – the making of Godfather Ferguson, in eight and a half episodes.

5.12.87: QPR 0 UNITED 2

For Reds stuffed into the prehistoric away enclosure at Loftus Road, the pre-match talk was not of football but of pub crawls, specifically the spectacular week-long tour of Manchester's niteries by Messrs. Whiteside and McGrath. United's greatest drinkers had truly excelled themselves this time, reaching such a state that they were relieved Fergie was keeping track of their progress with an A-to-Z: "they were glad at least I knew where they were because they had no idea" Alex quipped. Neither was fit to play: despite the Reds' victory, it marked the beginning of the end for the old brigade. Within 18 months, Strachan, Olsen and Moran had joined Norm 'n' Paul in the exodus from Old Trafford, a quintet who epitomized Big Ron's Cavaliers to be replaced by a hard new breed of Fergie Roundheads. The promised Glorious Revolution had finally arrived.

United actually finished the season in second, setting an Old Trafford record for the fewest defeats in the process but Fergie had seen enough: "this set of players had peaked and I knew they would never win the Title." We had all been expecting the Purge for some time. When Alex arrived, the contrast with Ron could hardly have been greater. In place of tans, jewellery and wideboy suits came blazers, regulation haircuts and the moral rigour of Scottish Protestantism. The days of the O.T. Boozers' Social Club were clearly numbered. Of Ron's boys, to whom Atkinson had allegedly got too close, only Robson and the returning prodigal Hughes were to survive the ensuing cull. The howls from the terraces as boyhood heroes were handed tickets to the glue factory were raucous – and enduring, as several of the discarded were saved by other Clubs en route and revived for years' more service. Strachan, in particular, must have enjoyed his 1992 vengeance. Much later, Fergie would paw the ground sheepishly and concede *sotto voce* that he may have been a bit hasty in one or two cases, especially as the squad soon became so emaciated that you could see all its ribs. Nevertheless, the Godfather had revealed his first traits: a patient fairness in allowing players plenty of time to make their pitch and a chilling ruthlessness in wielding the scythe when his mind was made up, deaf to the screams of horrified observers. Dismantling a runners-up side whilst sitting in football's hottest seat took some *cojones, amigo.*

1.1.89: UNITED 3 LIVERPOOL 1

Ah, sweet Scouse-smashing memories. For any eighties-boy Red, this was one of the best. As Fergie began reassembling the United jigsaw, apparently without a nice picture on the lid from which to work, we plunged relegation-wards; hit, too, by a mammoth injury crisis, we faced Liverpool at one of their many peaks live on telly. We prepared for another miserable bank holiday but instead witnessed a roasting of the dustbin-dippers that we'd never forget. Special enough in itself, of course, but a historic marker too. For Ferguson had the courage to throw a collection of raw kids into the team and gave them free reign – Sharpe, Robins, Martin, Beardsmore and, er, Ralphie Milne. Now there's nothing that excites a true Red more than the sight of a bunch of fresh, thrilling kids in shorts getting hot and sweaty doing their stuff for United, if you see what I mean. The addition of Gill, Graham and Wilson ten days later at QPR completed the full complement of what came to be known as 'Fergie's Fledglings' and together they illuminated an otherwise dank and dreary season. Two of the lads actually scored at Loftus Road, securing a replay on a night that conjured up memories of Docherty's Kids and even Busby's Babes. For the best part of two months, they kept the team afloat; typically, when the big boys returned, they got us knocked out of the Cup – with help from Brian Hill – and our season was over. The outstanding image of 88/89 remained young, gawky Russell Beardsmore, slamming the third into the Liverpool goal at the Stretford End; thanks for the memories, kids.

In the end, only Sharpe and Robins made it in the big-time. Injury, bad luck and loss of form accounted for the rest. Looking back objectively, Fergie remarked that they were never quite good enough for a Red future; tellingly, he also noted that they weren't 'his' kids but were inherited from Ron, with the exception of Sharpe. However, as we were soon to discover, Fergie had already committed himself to upholding the dearest Red tradition, that of cultivating youth. Long before he took his axe to the old first-teamers, he had already revamped our decrepit scouting system and begun devoting much of his time to the pursuit of young excellence. On New Year's Day '89, he had shown us his intent: as the 90s progressed, he produced the results. Giggs, Scholes, the Nevilles. Nicky Butt, Beckham ... Fergie's Fledglings Mark Two, as promised.

9.12.89: UNITED 1 PALACE 2

By now, Fergie had more than three years on the meter and what had we to show for it? Three months before, City had beaten us by a score I can't quite remember; we were at the start of a four month run without a home win; we were playing the worst football seen since Sexton; every other Ferguson buy was turning out to be a dud. Incredibly, relegation became a realistic possibility. Back in '74, when The Doc took us down, few clamoured for his dismissal. We could see what he was trying to do long-term, we had faith in his ability to produce eventual success, we could see the finished picture on the jigsaw box lid. But as United, bereft of the dropped hero Hughes, hoofed up long balls, misplaced passes and got turned over by these nondescript suburbanites, J-stand had had enough. "Fergie Out" came the cry; as the banner put it, "Enough excuses – ta ra Fergie." The manager raced home and hid, no longer willing to face the press, the fans, the world. The end was nigh, or so it seemed.

Somehow, the High Noon Cup shoot-out with Cloughie was won, ironically aided by a vibrant travelling Red Army, ninety per cent of whom wanted Fergie's testes on a platter; we stumbled and staggered onto a Cup run. Still, at Millwall in February, Red Issue's Chris Robinson "wanted us to lose, so that we could rid ourselves of Ferguson"; we won – for the first time in the league since November – and the monster lived on. Through sheer grit and determination rather than skill, we made it to the Cup Final. Red Issue sardonically labelled the Wembley event "Alex-Aid: eleven footballers try to keep Fergie out of the dole queue." For the fans, only a Cup win would be enough to warrant Ferguson's continuance in office. The Fledgling Martin duly won it for his boss and, grudgingly, another season's grace was granted. Never has the cliché 'a turning point' been more apt. Behind the scenes, however, the Godfather's one-to-one charisma had already secured his future long before the Final. As Jim White, author of 'Are You Watching Liverpool?' explains: "when Alex talks to you personally, he makes you feel like you are the most important thing in his world. His sincerity and integrity are overwhelming; he almost always knows how to get through to every variation of personality. He could convince you of anything." Martin Edwards and Bobby Charlton were under the spell. By guaranteeing Ferguson his future, they gave him his chance to work his man-to-man magic on the players. And within three years, the Sorcerer had all the players he wanted, dancing to the direction of his wand. For the fans, this was the sort of egg on our faces that we didn't mind licking off.

20.10.90: UNITED 0 ARSENAL 1

A twenty man brawl, if more handbags than fists, was just the sort of top entertainment we all love. The passionate, driven scrapper that is Alex Ferguson had demanded: "I insist that my teams have this quality ... huge, great fighting hearts that just don't want to be beaten." The foppish, easily-dispirited, 80s United had gone, replaced by a blazing, hardened beast – and about time too. Later, United would unjustly be labelled a dirty, petulant, over-aggressive side, a product of the manager's lack of discipline but better that than a collection of gutless, bloodless creeps. Fergie fined a couple of our boys under fierce media pressure but was soon to regret doing so. From now on, discipline was to be internal and private; he was no longer prepared to sacrifice players on the black altar of press opinion. He required absolute loyalty and discretion from his players; it was only right that he should give the same in return. Moreover, collective responsibility was now to be the doctrine: "I will never betray my staff by marking down individual scapegoats for collective failure." Like Montgomery and his troops, there was some serious battle-hardened bonding going down here: manager and players tied themselves together around the Club standard, yelling "Come on then, we'll take you all." Red fans, genetically programmed to respond to such combative stuff, purred in appreciation.

Where once Fergie had been slated for persevering too long with the hapless and the cretins (*vide* Leighton, Milne, Donaghy), he now began to reap credit for standing by such hesitant debutants as Ince, Pally and Blackmore, who were all beginning to gel with the team. "I was tuned into the players' psychological breakthroughs ... because it was similar to my own experience beginning at United," he remarked. The Fergie learning curve was about to lurch skywards.

28.11.90: ARSENAL 2 UNITED 6

As Chris Robinson says, "this was the night it all came right, at last." Arsenal, Champions-to-be with only one league defeat, handed the heaviest drubbing in forty years by a side using wingers, break-neck speed and one-touch pass 'n' move. "It took him a long time to realise what sort of football we demanded," remarks Robinson "but this was no accidental discovery of the true way." Indeed: by dropping an in-form

Webb and rejigging the tactics, Ferguson had gambled astutely. He had found the pattern and the mechanism at last after years of apparently fruitless tinkering; now all he had to do was replace some of the dodgier metalwork to complete his lean, sharp killing machine. With added victories in this league cup run over Champs Liverpool and a soon-to-be Champs Leeds, Fergie had at least returned us to where we were at Big Ron's peak, able to beat anyone on our day. Once Giggs, Eric and Andrei had arrived, 'on our day' was to become every day. Still, as that year's Final demonstrated, and as gratuitously repeated in 1994's counterpart, Big Ron could yet teach Fergie a thing or two about big match tactics and selection ...

20.4.92: UNITED 1 FOREST 2

Or 'Black Monday' as it is sometimes known, when United blew half of their '92 Title chance, finishing the job at Upton Park two days later. During the nadir of 89/90, the team were christened 'Fergie's F*ckwits' by Red Issue; now, as we were struck dumb by a series of bizarre selection decisions that ruined our rhythm and style, Fergie himself stood accused of being the 'F*ckwit'. Some, more politely, settled for the appellation 'Tinkerbell', as Hughes and Andrei in particular were left seething on the sidelines at crucial junctures. Thankfully, in our Title-winning seasons, this Ferguson disease went into remission somewhat, the bitter lessons of '92 having been apparently learned well. But, like the demented sculptor who doesn't know when to stop chipping away, the old habits resurfaced last season as Andrei at Goodison, Cole at Anfield and Hughes at Upton Park all discovered. Cue the sound of shattering masonry as the Title edifice crumbled ...

He still suffers the odd tactical stuffing too, whether at the hands of Big Ron or, more emphatically, Johann Cruyff; he continues to have a touching but entirely misplaced faith in players' ability to adapt to different roles as evidenced by the long-running David May farrago. Then there's the question of his motivational tactics; back in '92, there was much gossip about him overdoing the teacup-chucking and 'Fergie Fury' performances which were said to produce a pressure overload on players. Jim White wonders whether his other psychological tactics and Henry V-style dressing-room speechifying have become too repetitive, hence suffering from the law of diminishing returns. Time will tell; as for the 'Fergie Fury' malarkey, the man himself says he's calmed down now – he only uses the threat of the teacups, not the action itself. Royal Doulton are in mourning ...

6.12.92: UNITED 2 CITY 1

Eric Cantona makes his home debut: his first touch is a brilliant defence-shattering through-ball. Within the month, Eric has inspired five and four-goal displays against Coventry and Spurs as United's Title-odds tumble. Ferguson's greatest-ever transfer gamble hits the jackpot, in the face of the Hansen-led Cassandras. The 26-year wait is over: the Double follows. Our favourite song for three years now? – "Fergie's Red And White Army". A rather different tune to "Fergie's Out" ...

Of course, Cantona was the catalyst, the final piece without which the rest would not work quite as beautifully. And yes, there was a large element of luck in our securing his services. Yet once again, there had to be a man there prepared to take the risk, to go with his purist football instincts, a man willing to take the chance of his empire being contaminated by the seepage from football's most mercurial personality. Signing Eric was what Cantona himself, a French existentialist, might have termed an 'acte gratuite' – a self-defining active challenge to the world that expresses your freedom and beliefs. How deserved it is that Ferguson should be the main beneficiary of Cantona's gifts.

There are, however, ten others in a team. Their success demonstrated two further facets of the Godfather's powers. Firstly, (*pace* David May) his transfer-market nouse has improved immeasurably. Secondly, his unique, one-to-one managerial style has proved its worth. Few managers risk taking anything other than a uniform, no-favours, collective approach to man-management. Fergie has the confidence in his own managerial ability to buck that trend. "He'll be sharp and stroppy with Sharpe and Keane, fatherly and solicitous with Giggs and Butt, reverential and indulgent with Eric and so on; he pulls out every stop to motivate each as an individual and in doing that has got the very best out of each," says White. Success is not universal, of course. Get it wrong with one man and the result can be resentment and estrangement, as has seemingly occurred with Kanchelskis. In general, however, White has no doubts: "Of all the managers, he is by far the most personally impressive and charismatic, impossible to typecast, impossible to resist." Alex had found the pattern, found the players and found his managerial method.

12.3.94: UNITED 3 CHARLTON 1

Schmeichel is sent off in a Cup tie, a decision almost incontestably correct. In now archetypal Fergie-team style, United blaze back to win with passion anyway but Fergie emerges to lambast the referee. The media piranhas dive in for a feeding frenzy – yet another hothead Fergie outburst, to go with his 'Jimmy Hill's a prat', 'Galatasaray should be closed down' and 'teams leave Anfield choking back the vomit.' If you need any more reasons as to why we now love the man, look no further. He thinks, talks and reacts like one of us, like a true Red. No room for 'objectivity', for 'mature consideration' or for being 'a good loser' – he shoots from the hip, defends the indefensible and takes defeat as badly as McEnroe. Yes! This is exactly what we want from a United manager. We expect the impossible from our leader, in many ways. We want a Busbyesque father-figure to respect, a street-fighting hard case to empathize with and a football-loving connoisseur to tantalize all our senses. Ferguson, somehow, does the lot. Again, he is unusual amongst managers in that he makes almost no effort to cosy up to the press corps or, indeed, the world at large. Amidst the vulturish hacks, he is the soul of discretion, offering favours to few. All he cares about is United's staff and players: the rest of the world's existence is merely to be tolerated.

As we spent most of 94/95 behind the battlements, dominated by the siege mentality, what a man to have to hold us together as we huddled for comfort around the Red flag. Naturally, the siege might not have been so harsh had Ferguson's attitude not alienated so many outsiders in past years but we don't mind. We like it in here, repelling barbarians outside Old Trafford's walls. No-one likes us and we really don't care: we've got Alex and Eric, what more could we desire?

16.3.94: UNITED 5 WEDNESDAY 0

Eight episodes done: this is the half. To be precise, the first half against the Owls, when United scored four and threatened ten. Everything Ferguson has worked for was on display, whether in the commitment, the one-touch movements, the outrageous charges forward or the superb goals. 1994/95 might have witnessed the return of some unpleasant side-effects of Fergie's rule, from the tinkering and tactical botches to the transfer errors, but we'll all be turning up once more in 95/96 in the hope of being privileged enough to see more football like this – Ferguson-style.

If Ferguson is the Godfather, then Matt Busby was God himself: the late founder of the modern dynasty will never be replaced as the ultimate supremo. Alex, however, at least sits at his right hand. Recently he has talked of retirement, handing over the family to Brian Kidd or Bryan Robson but whatever they achieve they will be hard pressed to match the cinematically dramatic story of the Ferguson Years. There still remains the quest for the European Cup, which would be a fitting conclusion for the man once described thus: "He has the best qualities of all his predecessors; the decency and application of O'Farrell, the scholarliness of Sexton, the fun and humour of Docherty and the awareness and approachability of Atkinson." With a European Cup on the sideboard, an added reference to the best of Busby would be warranted too. For the modern Fergie's Red and White Army, it would be the least he'd deserve.

(First published in 'FourFourTwo', July 95)

FERGIE's TACTICAL MASTERCLASS - Part Two

In Part One of this series (available on MUFC Video for £18.99 with free Ryan Giggs tampon remover), we saw our manager expound the virtues of five-in-midfield, as seen at Upton Park, and five-in-defence as witnessed at Villa Park. We also learned how, when things don't go right, NEVER blame the system you picked but say that the players were shit instead.

Today, Alex unveils some new formations that might see action this year.

A) The "One-Nine-One".

"As youse all know, I am very concerned about 'swamping', especially away from home. I don't like risking our midfield getting over-run and it seems from what happened at West Ham that five-in-the-middle just isna enough. So when we're up for a battle this year, I'm going for nine in midfield to be sure, in three rows of three and all holding hands so we keep our shape. Whoever's upfront must also be prepared to chase back. Stevie Bruce will stay in defence as I'm convinced his timing, speed and touch are as good as when he was 25, just like I'm convinced that David May is a model of versatility.

Youse will notice that a 1-9-1 means we won't actually have a permanent goalkeeper but as I said to Peter Schmeichel at the Nou Camp, sometimes youse got to sacrifice yourself for the team. So we'll play fly goalie, with Choccy McClair running back from his lone upfront role to cover. His workrate's amazing, he covers every blade of grass etc. etc ...

B) The "Five-One-Four".

This might be the one we'll be going for in home games. My excellent new five-at-the-back which we practised so successfully in the Midlands will feature David May at sweeper, proving how versatile he is – and you need someone totally reliable and nerveless back there.

Nicky Butt, as I've said before, will be the best midfielder in the galaxy by Christmas. I have no doubt that he will rise to the challenge of being our only midfield player in this formation and will enjoy showing how right I was to sell Paul Ince, who only ever *seemed* to be our sole midfield star.

C) "The Whirl"

This isn't quite the same as that thing the Brazilians and Dutch did in the 70s but it'll be just as exciting. When the kids are having no joy, we can abandon 4-4-2 and switch to this which basically involves playing the natural game the kids learned at school. Therefore all eleven will rush madly around in a whirling pack chasing the ball, refusing to pass it, dribbling as far as they can go before falling over and grazing their knees. It will mystify the opposition and I'd like to stress that this is NOT the same system we used in the late 80s.

D) The "V" Formation.

We'll be using this against Everton and Inter Milan. Basically, May will be the pivot at the back with the two legs of the "V" stretching out to Giggsy and Lee on the wings. The message will be clear – a big V-sign f*ck off to those bastards Ince and the Russian from the whole team, including those who went to Incey's farewell party you'll notice. It'll leave the space in the middle to draw them in: then Roy and the boys will close in and kick the shit out of them. Not that I'm at all paranoid or defensive about the summer sales, of course ....

Look out for part three in the series, entitled "Fergie's Euro Tactical Triumphs", which will be broadcast in its entirety during the four minute slot after Channel 4 News.

(Sep. 95)

THE LONE GUNMAN AT THE O.T. CORRAL

In the wake of January's astonishing megadeal, 'Cole & Cantona' looked set to supplant Blackburn's S.A.S. as the Premiership's most mouth-watering strike force. But as any pessimistic United fan who was at the Crystal Palace game might testify, the Dream Duo is in danger of becoming a nightmare that could wreck both this and next season for Manchester United. Cole's performance was worrying enough without the sensational assault perpetrated by Cantona bringing further woe to all Reds. Close observers of the Old Trafford scene might claim to have seen this coming; it seems that United's strikers, both complex and private loners, are carrying some heavy emotional baggage which is threatening to overwhelm them. In Cantona's case, his very career is now in peril – but what of Andy Cole, the man now left to carry the attacking burden?

Something sinister began to happen up on Tyneside within a week of the Cole deal. After the first initial shocked horror stage had passed and the Toon Army used the televised Man. United game to rally behind Keegan, some Geordies began to refer to the affair as 'The Great Con-trick', adding the odd knowing wink for good measure. On Sky TV, Brian Woolnough put it more bluntly: "There's something fishy about this deal." Attentive Mancunians, already concerned about the probable loss of Hughes and the fact that Cole was on a goal-free run, could only be further alarmed by this and the rumours emerging from Tyneside. Just what had Fergie bought – surely not a £7 million pig-in-the-poke? Unhappy visions of Gary Birtles materialized in front of Red eyes ...

The nub of the doubt was this: had Newcastle really let Cole go because, in fact, he was just too much to handle? And had his personal problems, whatever they were precisely, combined to make his current loss of form permanent? Exactly what are these personal difficulties anyway? Cole was already notorious for being the most homesick player in the North – his bust-up with Keegan in the autumn of '93 and his subsequent AWOL flight back to the capital are well-documented but were by now supposed to be well behind him. However, you can find plenty of Geordies who'll tell you otherwise. Davey James, a Toon fanatic who specializes in monitoring his heroes around town, notes: "I never see him out and about – and if I do, it's not with another Newcastle player. He's just not the 'lads night out' type, I reckon." Cole was living a small-town life in Crook, happy with the company of his massive CD collection and the telephone, but far away from the people who mean most to him. Girlfriend Shirley, who's expecting a baby, still lives in North London where she's studying for a degree; his family are still in their Nottingham base whilst best friend Ian Wright remains firmly ensconced at Highbury. Crook could be a million miles away. In a 'Manchester Evening News' profile, Louise Taylor talked darkly of Cole's supposed 'social withdrawal' from the Club's personnel and how he seemed to be distancing himself from the world at large. Then 'The Guardian' remarked upon the mysterious quality of a recent Keegan quote: "I've heard a lot of nasty things said about Andy in recent weeks but I've never found him to be a problem." Hmm ... the plot thickens, Watson.

What United fans will want to know is whether Cole is going to be bringing this apparent unsettled unhappiness with him to Old Trafford or is the move the one thing that can put a smile back on the increasingly sullen striker's face? Manchester is, at least, much closer to both London and Nottingham; then there's the comforting presence of the recently-befriended Paul Ince, if Giggsy can bear to be parted from his soul-mate for a few weeks. Above all, there's the manager, well-used to dealing with melancholic home-bird types. However, if Andy's troubles run deeper than mere homesickness or being tired of Geordie life, perhaps all that won't be enough.

The real question might be whether Cole is ever going to be happy in the North as a whole, being a Southern soulboy having to cope with the Northern mentality. Apparently, one of the final straws at St. James' Park was the racist abuse his family got when they came to see him play – as John Barnes once found, such terrace expressions of opinion tend to put rather more forcefully up North than in the more cosmopolitan London (*pace* Upton Park.) Being just about the only black face in town may not have been the most pleasant experience for the Crook-bound Cole; at least Manchester might offer more of a spiritual home in that respect. Still, for the time being, the image of Cole via his clothes, mannerisms and tastes speaks of an unassimilated Southerner enduring a Northern exile – even Manchester might not be 'sophisticated' enough to make him a good home.

If all this psychology does not give sufficient cause for concern, how about a spot of physiology? The saga of the Cole injury back in autumn '94 – an apparent case of shin-splints – was pock-marked by constant Cole denials that he was suffering from any such malady: "It's just a muscle strain" was Cole's constant refrain. The St. James' doctors cleared his return and assured Keegan that there'd be no long term damage but, as is well known, he never reproduced his best after that break. How long will Old Trafford have to wait to see that penalty-box lightning strike with weekly regularity once more? There have been many players down the years who, if not having their careers terminated by a particular injury, have at least never been the same since. United's £7 million gamble is riding on the hope that Cole has not joined that sorry group.

Assuming that Cole is physiologically sound, then it may be the psychology that matters above all. United have, down the years, had perhaps more than their fair share of personality clashes and clique-factionalism. All Reds pray that whatever the dressing-room breakdown is these days, Andy Cole emerges as a happier soul and consequently a better player, for any one of seven million reasons ...

(First published in 'The Game', Feb. 1995)

ANDY COLE - AN APOLOGY

It has been brought to our attention that many observers may have got entirely the wrong impression of our attitude to Mr. Andrew Cole. Due to, er, typographical errors and general media distortion, Reds in the past have appeared to view young Andy as any of the following: a one-season wonder; a talentless goal-hanger; a gun-toting wideboy; a poor man's Chris Eubank; a general Geordie-loving arrogant twat of the first order.

Naturally, none of this was ever true and we would like to assure everyone that our opinion of Mr. Cole has always been consistent, to whit that he is a fine upstanding young man of supreme athletic gifts, one of our favourite and most-admired players of recent years and a credit to his ethnicity and family. When, for example, we sang "you'll never play for England" at him up at St. James' Park, all we meant to express was our view that he was too good for Venables' outfit and instead deserved to play for Brazil.

Anyway, we hope we have clarified our position on this and cleared up any misunderstandings. Incidentally, in the spirit of friendship, may we direct traumatized Toons to seek solace from fellow north-eastern sheepshaggers at Elland Road whom we understand to have had some experience of this sort: how painful it must be to have Fergie plunge his hand into your chest and rip out your heart, tee-hee ....

(Feb.95)

"EE-AY PADDIO"

That's one of the lead tracks on Pete Boyle's next album, along with "Wake Up, Paddy": they were the first two Pete insisted on recording for "The Red Album 2". Ask him why he's temporarily shifted the focus of his devotion from King Eric to Prince Paddy Crerand, Pete simply replies "respect is due – by public demand." Apparently, so many Reds asked the Boyle to immortalize Crerand in song that he felt duty-bound to do so. In a recent fanzine poll, Paddy was voted Red of the Year; in Gothenberg, he was virtually mobbed by well-wishers on the Allevyn and had to duck out down backstreets. At a Club where every individual has at least some critics, no-one I know has ever heard a word said against him. Although he'd probably slap me for sacrilege in saying so, he has moved into the Premiership of the Respected to take his place alongside Sir Matt and Eric.

How has this happened? After all, he hasn't played for a quarter-century, his main public visibility these days being via radio commentary: many of his fans are too young to have ever seen him play. The country is full of ex-United pundits – and it's not as though he was our greatest-ever player either, his being name absent from the Holy Trinity litany of Best, Law and Charlton.

Ah, but therein lies the rub, already exposed. To describe his current standing as that of just another media pundit is laughably inadequate, as we shall see. First, let us remember where he's coming from. The cognoscenti of Red history and those who were actually there during that swinging, seismic decade will tell you that Crerand was the key to the success of that great side – and in some ways, the embodiment of its special qualities. It is a happy co-incidence, given the way his personal life developed, that as a professional he was so reminiscent of Busby the player. The two of them epitomized that classic model of football history – the cultured, civilized Scottish half-back who thrived on skill and intelligence rather than mere pace and force. Never physically quick, a supposed fault that cost him his place under O'Farrell, his speed was all in the mind and touch. For vision, instinct, courage and pure craft, there was no-one better. Decades before we were enthralled by Eric's ability to see and execute the ball that all others were blind to, Paddy was knocking them off every few minutes. But then, genius was in ample supply at Old Trafford then: only at mid-60s United could such powers be taken for granted. The roll-call of the Holy Trinity should, to be accurate, have been expanded to a quartet: some will tell you that although United could still function when one of the golden trio was absent, the loss of Crerand was always to be keenly felt.

He took a few weeks to settle at United but once his man of the match performance in the '63 Cup Final was under his belt, he transformed United into Title challengers and winners. Fittingly, given his latter-day support of Eric, his impact and role was Cantonesque – by becoming the brain of the team, in Bestie's phrase, he acted as the alchemic catalyst that turned Old Trafford gold. He too displayed the fight and temper of a man who won't accept injustice, perhaps a product of a superior morality that places a man's own moral code above those imposed by lesser mortals – like refs and administrators in general. Whatever, that battling brave commitment was precisely what we all want from our midfield generals. It was Crerand who, in the devastated aftermath of European semifinal defeat in '66, rose from the dressing room bench to promise Matt that we would win the '67 Title and from there the European Cup – he did as much as anyone to ensure he kept his promise to his 'adopted father'.

The relationship with Busby was always a key element in his life. Matt, drawn to street-wise, larger than life characters, would have liked him anyway: add to that the Crerand integrity, honesty and decency which Busby always looked for in himself and others and it comes as no surprise that the Crerands were always favourite guests at Matt's modest Chorlton residence. Moreover, they had both been forged by similar life experiences; neither born with silver spoon in mouth, both proud upholders of a Scottish/Irish Catholic ancestry, both fierce individualists who nevertheless overcame the collective Anglo and Protestant bigotries ranged against them. When Crerand explains his relative lack of Scottish caps in terms of the bias against Celtic/United Catholics, it is not an 'excuse' but the plain truth. And when you hear the Dunphy story about Paddy throwing a pint in the face of a reserve who was singing the 'The Sash', you understand that his sentiments run deep. He doesn't just passively belong to a tradition – he actively defends it. So it is with Paddy and United: if you're not prepared to man the barricades at moments of strife, then you've become part of the problem. Crerand never looked for trouble – life was always for enjoying to the full – but when the calls came, he took up the trident. Benfica in '68, The Doc in court, the Red-hating media in '95: they've all felt Paddy's prongs ....

It's a tantalising historical 'what-if' that Crerand was considered by Busby as his successor in 1969 before McGuiness got the job; Paddy was playing too well to be moved upstairs in those pre-player/manager days. Throughout that often tortuous decade, Paddy was one of the few to emerge with clean hands from the behind-the-scenes skullduggery. Typically, he behaved with Busbyesque impeccability. As usual, his judgments were spot-on: Wilf got the job too soon and under the wrong conditions, O'Farrell simply wasn't the right man for the post in the first place. Both managers dropped Paddy but unlike other ageing heroes, he wasn't motivated by this to become a back-stabber: neither ex-manager will finger Paddy as a malcontent. The Doc, notoriously, engineered Paddy out through a series of unsubtle slights and snubs: he paid for it later, firstly when Paddy alerted Matt to the Brown situation, later when he responded to Willie Morgan's libel action call to arms. It was a rare direct intervention in United politics but, in retrospect, one that was wholly justified. Taking up a managerial role at Northampton, Crerand was his usual no-nonsense self; facing a Board he believed had reneged on previous assurances, he simply cleared his desk and walked out. If they'd assumed he was the archetypal duck 'n' dive, give-and-take merchant, they were hugely mistaken.

Throughout the Eighties, Paddy did most of the usual ex-player stuff: he ran a pub in Alty, got involved in a travel firm with Big Norm, did a spot of hospitality at OT and so on. But fundamentally, he remained a fan, going to as many games as possible and taking advantage of radio commentator offers to combine work with pleasure. So he'd joined the punditocracy – hardly remarkable. Yet as the years have gone on, he has increasingly stood out from that over-populated and generally mediocre class. Passionate, opinionated, utterly biased, highly observant and unafraid to offend with the truth, he was every Red's choice of ideal match companion. As time went on, other would-be standard-bearers for the legacy of United have fallen by the wayside: Law on mundane autopilot for ITV, Bobby lost to the clutches of the Board, Best staggering about over bottles and birds in between rank videos. Paddy's the last authentic voice from another era.

However, it's what he says and what he stands for that matters. As his voice became more widely sought-after by the media and the football world, what makes him special became clearer. Because he talks to us, the fans – and, more importantly, listens – he is in tune with the spirit of United like few others. Because he is genuine, open and democratic in the broadest sense of the world, we seek him out: and because of his reputation as player and man, the Club have no option but to defer to him too. He is able to straddle the worlds of 'official' and 'unofficial' United – thus remaining both hugely well-informed and highly influential – in a way that no-one else can. Even when supposedly constrained by the self-censorship of 'official' United, for example in his Man U Mag column, he says what no-one else would dare say with complete forthrightness. He's probably not cynically sly enough to realise and exploit the fact that he can do this because his status makes him virtually untouchable – he just does what comes naturally, that is talking honestly and without guile or fear.

So we have learned to appreciate that in United's internal debates, he is the only man of stature who will willingly put our case and do so because he knows the issues and will make his own mind up. But when it's United against the world, he alone can speak for all of us, Club and fans. The Cantona Affair saw Paddy at his best, stepping into the breach when no-one else could or would dare. That awful night, as our coaches crawled away from the scene, Paddy took up our standard on radio and put all the pro-Eric arguments that later became our common currency. For 24 hours he stood virtually alone, reviled by the rest of Britain for his defence of our God, as he appeared wherever he could to stuff some common sense down the throats of the lynch-mob. He stood fast on that beach-head, clutching the Red Flag, deflecting the flack until the rest of us could catch him up and support him: for that and his continued campaign on behalf of Eric alone, he would deserve all our thanks.

Many of the traditions and qualities that United had under Busby have long gone. The old brotherly club is now an inhuman plc behemoth, the ground a sanitized plastic family playground, the newer fans often a strange breed, uneducated in the ways of the Reds. Links to the soul of the Club, that of the departed Sir Matt, should be cherished wherever they are found. A friend of mine who's been lucky enough to get to know Paddy well thinks his strength and popularity derive from a simple quality: "he lives life on the Busby principle – they share so many characteristics and beliefs that the respect Paddy is held in is no surprise at all." When we sing "United we love you", I often wonder what we mean by 'United'. The fans? Too many are entirely unlovable. The ground? Give me the 1976 version any day. The players? Heroes today, villains tomorrow. The Club? Edwards, Merrett & Co – are you joking? No: I think 'United' is a spiritual concept, not a physical one. It means something about the way you behave, the way you play, the way you think, the way you support. That spirit, occasionally, is visible in certain individuals. Matt was one such being – and Paddy Crerand is another.

(First published here: thanks to JF, ED, PB))

"EE-AY, PADDIO"

by Peter Boyle, from the 'Red Album 2'.

Oh he's United through and through
He showed Nobby what to do
He took Denis out at nights
Then helped Georgie in those fights
Played with passion in our team
Helped Sir Matt with his Euro-dream
Was so tough for all those years
Got sent off but never fears ...

Chorus:
PADDY, PADDY, PADDY CRERAND
GLASGOW BORN AND GLASGOW BRED
WAS A CELT FOR MANY YEARS
BUT MOST OF ALL HE WAS A RED

A working-class bloke
Of which he's mighty proud
Stood up tall and shouted out loud
For the Glasgow streets and those Gorbals flats
The down-to-earth upbringing
Just like Sir Matt's
Nowadays his passion remains
To commentate he now gets paid
Nailed his colours to the post
When he backed Eric more than most
So raise your glasses, down that beer
Think of Paddy, be proud and cheer
Forever and ever respect is due
To Paddy the Scot – but always Man U.

"OOH-AY, DAVID MAY"

At the end of the 94/95 season, 'FourFourTwo' ran a series of player profiles under the title 'The Boy's A Bit Of a Disappointment' and there was little surprise that United's resident City fan headed the list. The author tried his hardest to resist breaking the rule that you don't criticize your own in public but just couldn't stop himself. Forty thousand fellow sufferers may well sympathize.

My girlfriend, who has a weird feminine way of prejudging players, took one look at David May on his arrival and pronounced "Ginger, curling hair and freckles – he's no good." If only Fergie could pick up some of this female intuition malarkey, for as we all now know, Davey boy is not exactly this year's Number One Megastore poster. Indeed, as his harsher 'Red Issue' critics would contend, the points we lost due to his nightmare showings at full-back have been as instrumental as King Eric's absence in our losing the Title. The chant we had prepared for him of 'Ooh-Ay, David May' has sadly usually been heard in only the most ironic of tones.

Back in those carefree days of August '94, when King Eric roamed free, Paul Parker was fit and Rovers were beaten at Wembley, life was so much sweeter. How we revelled in capturing May from the enemy camp, outwadding Blackburn's sugar daddy for once and leaving a dirty great hole in the Rovers defence. How delightful too that Rovers fans should be so hugely miffed at the blow to their pride; even as late as January, they were still bellowing 'Judas' at him on the Old Trafford touch-line, bunging thirty pieces of silver five pences towards him for good measure. As usual, the alarmingly inbred Lancastrians were rather slow on the uptake – many of us had already decided May was clearly a Dalglishean agent sent to destroy us from within.

He made a terrible start and from then it was all downhill. Revealing that he had been a City fan as a teenager was bad enough without him going on to name his Fantasy Football team 'M.C.F.C'. We can safely assume that had May not become a footballer, a career in public relations would not have been his next choice. Bluenoses at United are supposed to repent their sins upon signing for us, not continue shamelessly to flaunt them. All in all, a bad omen: City fans at United usually come to grim ends as Mark Robins and Billy Garton both discovered.

Still, we could have forgiven him this unfortunate accident of Blue birth had he not proceeded to offer definitive proof that your standard English centre-half is about as adaptable as a three-pin plug and about as much use in Europe too. Now admittedly even demi-gods like Pally and Bruce would struggle at full-back but at least they'd be able to keep their heads above water. Poor David simply drowned, all at sea when more than ten yards away from his comfy centre-half home. On those occasions when he was actually in position on the flanks instead of loitering without intent in the box, he succeeded in making every trundling journeyman wide player look like a dazzling, dashing winger in the Giggs and Best mould. Within weeks he had become the Skoda of English defenders: everything else can overtake it with ease, no-one else wants to own one and it's the butt of every bar-room joke going. At times, he resembled a demented owl, his head swivelling wildly as if through 360 degrees as he tried to locate the ball and opponent. As teams started to cash in by playing two or three left-wingers against him, unchallenged crosses whizzed over from his corner with depressing regularity. Only the domineering presence of Pallister saved us from further ignominy.

Not that it was all Davey's fault. Ferguson. typically, refused to concede for months what even single-cell amoeba beyond Alpha Centauri had long since realised – that even Andy Cole would make a better full-back than May. By then, of course, it was too late. The damage had been done. On a grisly Ullevi night, David reached his nadir. Blomqvist roasted May to such an extent that watching Reds chanted 'off, off' whenever the ref had words with the hapless creature. When 'Red Issue' put together a piece entitled 'Ten Reasons Why United Lost In Europe', the editor had to be physically restrained from typing 'David May' ten times. It wasn't just that May had been atrocious either, as Ferguson had to take some of the blame for playing him out of position yet again. It was also that his attitude seemed suspect. In this very organ, Rob Shepherd noted darkly that on the plane home, all United players looked deathly, with some appearing to be in shock. Not so David; Shepherd spotted him laughing and joking, seemingly without a care in the world. The fanzine "United We Stand" put this in their next issue and for many, May was now *persona non grata.*

We haven't seen much of him since. He had a couple of chances at centre-half and still wasn't much good, heading the ball in all directions but safe ones with his eyes closed like an eight year old girl. He did have a good game at Palace and even scored, allowing us to sing 'Ooh-Ay' in earnest at last – for we never criticize him loudly at games, ever-optimistic that he might improve. But that was the night of Cantona's kung-fu, when the surreal and bizarre held sway – you could file a decent May display under one of those headings ...

Of course, we pray the boy comes good, especially with Brucey heading for his bus pass. In the meantime, anyone got a spare centre-back to sell us? Part-exchange?

(First published in 'FourFourTwo', May 95)

You've seen 'Giggsy's Soccer Skills' now enjoy ... 'PLAY THE MAY WAY' - with new boy, David

1) The offside trap

"I've been trying out my new secret method of playing the offside trap which always seems to get the fans going. As soon as Brucey shouts, the other three lads step up smartly but I leg back towards the corner flag as quick as poss. and try to hide from the linesman. Then, if the attackers beat the trap, I can suddenly materialize from nowhere and make the saving tackle! Er.. or not, as the case may be. Obviously, we're still ironing out a few flaws here; I might have to dye my hair cos Mr. Linesman always seems to spot my bright ginge-minge barnet. But the lads seem to appreciate it in their special-sense-of-humour way – Brucey always shouts over a cheery, "May, you wanker".

2) Tackling wingers

"With these new FIFA laws, you've really got to watch yourself haven't you? What I advise all young players is to follow my example – when a winger comes up to you with the ball, don't go in there feet flying. In fact, it's better not to go in at all. Sort of jump about from left to right, hold him up for a few seconds just long enough for all his colleagues to arrive in the box, then let him go. Brucey and Pally will deal with the cross won't they? No need to make rash challenges and get booked – a good pro doesn't need to get suspended and miss those win bonuses does he? I think Peter appreciates all the extra handling practice this tactic gives him – he always shouts a merry "You ginger twat" which I think is a Danish pregnant goldfish. Crazy guy!"

3) Covering your colleagues

"It's essential to support your central defensive team-mates when play pulls them out of position, so I'm always ready to get across and stand in for Pally or Stevey at a second's notice. Funnily enough, I find myself needing to do this more and more, drifting cleverly into the box for up to 90% of the game. The lads are always pleased to see me help out in the thick of things and they certainly don't think I've forgotten I'm supposed to be at full back – Pally's Geordie humour is such a laugh, he always greets me in the box with a hearty "Get out of the way, you dick".

4) Overlapping up the wing

"This is the easiest thing I've had to adjust to at Old Trafford. Mr Ferguson just told me to watch Paul Parker play, do whatever he does and I'll make a good fullback yet. So when I get the ball on the wing, I leg forward, look up meaningfully several times, then either hoof it to the opposing goalie or into the stands. The tactical purpose of this escapes me but I always do what I'm told. Keano loves it when I do this – he always rushes over and spits in my face. I think this is a quaint Irish sign of appreciation for the best players, like that bloke Kubilay.

5) Handling the media

"Obviously this is so important at such a big club. I always try to be cleverly humorous in my interviews. So when I was on TV with Brucey next to me, I said "Why don't you pack your bags and leave, Stevey?" It was so funny! Brucey didn't know what to say but he gave me a playful kick in the Achilles tendon later to show we were mates. Actually, it was a bit hard come to think of it. Likewise, when Man U Mag asked me to name my fantasy footie team, I called it Man City! Hilarious or what? This is what my new intellectual friend Choccy called "irony". A United fan who saw me the next day shouted "Bluenose knobhead" at me which proved he'd got the joke and wasn't bad at this irony game either! It's a laugh a minute here you know.

(In the words of Terry Wogan to another David – Icke – "they're laughing at you, not with you, Dave.)

This great video is now available in a series along with "Corner-taking with Giggsy" and "Controlling You Rage the Keano Way" priced £37.99 with a limited edition (20,000) Fred the Red gonk thrown in for free.

(March 95)

SO THAT THE MEEK SHAN'T INHERIT THE EARTH ...

At the end of the 94/95 season, David Meek retired as the United correspondent for the "Manchester Evening News", a post he'd held since the Munich Disaster. Supposedly the doyen of the Old Trafford press pack, his final days were feted with awards, tributes and commemorations as he prepared to spend the rest of his days freelancing, a deal to columnize for the "Evening News" safely tucked in the wallet. But should United fans continue to regard him as the great omniscient Oracle of O.T., still the journalist to rely upon, to respect? The author thinks not.

Talk to any members of the United-watching press pack about David Meek and, for once, you'll get a uniformity of opinion: "nice bloke", "decent fella", "salt of the earth" and other such blandishments trip easily off the admittedly sometimes forked silver tongues. It's what they don't say that's interesting: never do you hear "top-flight writer", "tremendous story-breaker" or "fearless crusader" – in short, none of the epithets that hard-bitten hacks normally dream of earning. Curious, that.

But no more curious than the "News" reporter's job is to begin with, perhaps. Meek, as holder of the position throughout these decades of media explosion, has shaped this role to such a degree of concrete irrevocability that Stuart Mathieson and his successors would struggle to deviate from the appointed path, presuming that they would ever wish to do so. It's hard to over-exaggerate the centrality of the Meek Model in the lives of locally-based Reds. Not only are the match reports in the "News" and "Pink" read by the majority of Manc Reds, the mid-week news items are the primary sources of information for all, be they fans or other media. Then there's the radio and TV appearances, supplemented by whatever syndicated or commissioned articles can be rustled up in other papers and magazines, that allow for further comment, 'insight' and guidance, all gratefully hoovered-up by news-hungry fans. Add to that the unquantifiable tips and 'spin-doctoring' that may be given to other less privileged hacks behind the scenes – and the fact that MUFC is the most secretive club in Britain – and you can appreciate that the position of the "News" correspondent allows the incumbent enormous influence over the way United's affairs are perceived by the outside world. True, the phenomenal growth of tabloid interest in MUFC over recent years has meant that what were once local-only stories now appear on national back pages too; consequently, several national journalists are beginning to catch up with the "News" in terms of influence and access. Nevertheless, the "News" man remains 'primus inter pares', wielding an almost automatic credibility that the nationals have yet to earn.

Meek, however, always had one disadvantage compared with the tabloid guys. He was, essentially, on his own, solely responsible for the United coverage in the "News" and thus the individual answerable to both the Club and readers for his coverage. The tabloids have at least two United specialists each, normally a Mr. Nasty squatting in London, ever ready with an invented shock-horror story, balanced by a Mr. Nice up in Manchester, always prepared to give the Club the benefit of the doubt and happiest when running 'good news' pieces. That's a grossly simplistic synopsis of what are actually very Byzantine and unfathomable cross-relationships but the results are effective enough. Tabloid stories hostile to United that enrage the Club can be 'blamed' on London – the Manchester correspondents can then maintain their friendly links with favourite United sources by saying "it wasn't me, Guv."

The "News" man has no such luxury. Cross the Club in print and the consequences, in terms of the reporter being able to get his job done easily, can be awkward. Cross the readers, however, and what is the penalty? Say he runs a piece backing ticket price hikes, defending the Board and attacking complaining fans. Some fans will be angry; one or two might even get past the 'Postbag' guards and have a letter printed. So what? Where else is the Mancunian reader going to go for his United latest when the "News" has a monopoly? If the reporter is of the old-school type who never talks to or quotes local fans anyhow, then he has even less to worry about: in the pecking order of groups not to be offended, the fans come a long way behind the Manager, the Board and the players.

You can see where this is going now, can't you? Many years ago – twenty-three to be precise – there was a defining moment in the coverage of United by the "News". David Meek is now perceived to have run a very brave piece defending Frank O'Farrell during the last days of his benighted regime in which he argued that everyone, including those within the Club who were unhappy with Frank, should give the man more time rather than agitate for his dismissal. Meek pointed out that the McGuiness situation had been handled cack-handedly and that lessons should be learned: now was the time to issue a statement of support for Frank and accept that the Club as a whole was responsible for the current demise, not just O'Farrell.

The perception of bravery stems from the fact that, as many in Manchester's better-informed circles knew before the article appeared, the Board had already decided to sack O'Farrell two days previously. It looked as though Meek, who presumably knew this, disapproved and had gone as far as he could in public to make his disgust plain. Certainly that was the Club's view: the Board immediately informed Meek he was banned from the team coach and some difficult weeks followed for the hapless reporter. Hapless? Well, it turned out that he'd had no idea that the decision to sack O'Farrell had already taken place. Quite accidentally, through not being well-informed, he'd made himself look much more courageous than he'd surely ever intended – from a cock-up emerged a crusader.

Addicts of hypotheticals might like to conjecture as to how Meek might have behaved had he known O'Farrell was already dead in the water: more cynical students of his later career might contend that a "So long, Failure Frank – and thanks for Martin Buchan" would've been a likelier headline, if Meek's volte-face over Paul Ince last summer is the yard-stick. (Remember how one week he was lauding Ince for having topped the year's ratings chart and talking of his glittering future as next captain? Within the month, Ince was the bossy, too-big-for-his-boots liability as Meek implicitly backed Fergie's view that Ince had only played "four good games" that season. As Meek always boasts of his 'behind-the-scenes' knowledge, how come he didn't see fit to tell us about Ince's alleged failings long before his departure?) To be fair, the 1972 Meek Model seems to have been a patently courageous and independently-minded version. He wasn't cowed and refused to hide himself away, being justly rewarded by certain players and officials who continued to brief him quite openly. Eventually, relations warmed up once more and if Meek wasn't literally back on board the coach, he was at least back within the family fold as a Prodigal Son of sorts.

And therein lies the rub. The episode was a watershed but it could've been a moment of much different consequence. Brian Redhead, then editor of the "News", was outraged at the way the Club treated Meek and offered "to go to war" with United over this and the larger issues it raised. Meek was grateful but declined the bellicose option, preferring to work it out on his own. I spoke to Redhead about a year before his death and managed to make the subject come up. He ruminated on the episode and although he had nothing but praise for Meek's bearing throughout this little Cold War, wondered whether it might have been better after all to slug it out with United. I suggested that such a fight might have altered the way United-"News" relations were conducted forever – instead of the cozy alliance there seems to be between the two bodies, we might instead have benefited from a much healthier scenario of mutual scepticism and mistrust. Redhead didn't demur. Instead of reporters gratefully accepting the stories United choose to feed them, they would be forced to dig and forage and thereby give us stories of substance rather than bland PR-sheen news releases. Similarly, the Club would have to account for its deeds – or misdeeds – to properly inquisitive and impartial reporters rather than luxuriate in the contented knowledge that the last paper who'd ever give them a hard time is the "News".

Sadly, the aftermath of 1972 panned out very differently. Lessons appear to have been learned all round but not, I would contend, to the educational benefit of United fan readers. Think back over all the traumatic episodes at Old Trafford since then: three managerial sackings of course but also the myriad scandals and outrages that included boardroom battles, personal tabloid disgraces, controversial sales and purchases, rip-offs, libels, court cases, violence, exploitation, profiteering and so on. It's a cliché that life at Old Trafford resembles a soap opera but truly we host more drama and suspense than 'Brookie' and 'Corrie' combined. But can you recall any of these crises or debates featuring a campaigning "Evening News" at the forefront? How many serious stories that might embarrass MUFC have been broken by the "News"? How many articles can you recall that have backed a fans' movement against either the Board, management or a particularly unpopular player? Look through Crick & Smith's 'Betrayal of a Legend' and remind yourself of some of the activities engaged in by United's leaders – how many of those were even noticed, let alone criticized by the "News"? Judged on such a survey, who could blame any on-looker for thinking that the "News" – and, as their central player, David Meek – have been so reluctant to tackle the thornier issues that they appear to be nothing more than eunuchs at the Old Trafford harem? And who can blame Reds for holding their noses and turning to the tabloids *et al* for their United fix because they can't trust the "News" to give them the full picture? What happened to the old maxim "all the news that's fit to print" – when did the suffix "as long as it doesn't annoy Merrit/Ramsden/Fergie/Edwards" get appended?

If you don't like to dwell on ancient history, then let us stick to those events of the recent past for which you'd have expected our local paper and our local man to make the running. The outrage in Istanbul? – well done for top coverage to David Mellor and the fanzines. Commercialization and social engineering at Old Trafford? – Channel 4, Newsnight and the football magazines. Pursuing explanations for last summer's sales? – the Star and the Mirror. Reporting the important progress of the IMUSA? – well, every medium except the "News". The "Evening News" calls itself 'a friend dropping in': MUFC plc must think its the best friend they've ever had.

As the man at the helm, David Meek is the one who must answer for such a selection of material. He cannot plead ignorance of his readers' concerns, concerns which stretch to rather more than merely news of who is injured, who's in the team and what the manager thought of the latest performance. He has read the fanzines from almost the beginning; indeed, it was his pompous condemnation of 'Red Issue' that gave them their biggest sales surge ever. He does, therefore, know that his readers are interested in the greater, 'political' aspects of MUFC – he has simply chosen not to reflect them in his journalism. Having laid down this gold standard, he has set a course from which his successor has not yet shown any signs of daring to deviate. Such is the legacy of twenty-three years reporting of the 'old school' style, the school that Meek's admirers claim he personifies in excelsis. Personally, I think it's one of the few traditions around Old Trafford that I'd like to see the back of – but without a fundamental re-examination of their journalistic rigour at the "News", I suspect we're stuck with Meekism for some time to come.

Meek himself remains as much on the scene as ever. Indeed, his weekly "News" column gives him even more opportunity for opinionated grand-standing than ever although it is noticeable that the 'new school'-dominated world of the modern football press such as 'Goal' and 'Four-FourTwo' have not been rushing excitedly to him for copy. Freelancing is a tough old world for old school warriors and in the new fan-friendly media environment, being perceived to be an Establishment croney can't help.

Meek's treatment of the Independent Man Utd Supporters Association this year serves as a good case study to illustrate the thesis behind this piece. Before the argy-bargy over the summer sales rumbled onto the back pages, Meek had already made a couple of telling stumbles resulting partly from his continued reluctance to maintain the sort of meaningful dialogue with fans' bodies that national journalists tend to daily. On the Monday before Eric Cantona re-signed for United, Meek told his readers to expect the worst: he confidently predicted God would be pledging to Milan on the next 'Black Friday'. Unfortunately for Meek's credibility, the more informed fans already knew through our own sources that Eric would, in fact, be staying. The truth was a phone call away for the "News" but it was 10p they'd never bring themselves to spend. That same month, Meek penned a centre-page tribute to Martin Edwards in the 'Pink', glorying in the new 'Gold Trafford' and telling fans it was time to pay homage to our leader, whose fine stewardship had proved all the doubters wrong. The timing was hilarious – days before, the IMUSA had been formed precisely because dissatisfaction with MUFC had reached such an uncontainable peak, with the ticket price broken promises and the new ban on standing being the proverbial final straws. Meek appeared to be blissfully unaware of both the fans' mood and the sheer bad timing of his piece: never has a serious article produced such mirth.

Once the IMUSA was underway, Meek went in with the boot on four separate occasions, each time blundering to such an extent that he'd have been better off getting the boot itself to write the piece. That Meek was hardly hosting a ticker-tape welcome for the IMUSA was no surprise.

(Fans threatening to think and act for themselves, disturbing the cozy circle of Boardroom, dressing room and press box, promising to cut out media middle-men by using their own sources to get info to members? No thanks, lads.) That IMUSA was misrepresented quite appallingly on each occasion was almost to be expected, given that he never bothered to interview them first. That he should twice cause me in particular to consult libel lawyers in London was a bonus: in both instances, I was informed I could sue but graciously settled for reply articles and letters in the "News" and for the satisfaction of hearing that the Editor had to send out letters of apology to complaining readers.

So pardon me for not kneeling at the altar of Saint David as the rest of the football writers' world has done but give me Steve Curry or Jim White any day. If you are one of the many who were never that keen on Meek to begin with, don't waste time criticizing him for the trivial annoyances, the innumerable times he's repeated a bum steer from United and predicted the wrong team line-up or the fantastically bizarre player ratings that always seemed to give the ref and McClair twice their worth. What really matters is that he could have done so much for us, the readers, the long-suffering and often ally-less United hard-core. But when it mattered, when we needed support for our overwhelming sentiment against a particular decision or development, when we were desperate for the unvarnished inside story, David Meek wasn't truly there for us. He now tells us, to paraphrase a recent column, that he is free to say the unsayable, to lay into issues that the Club themselves cannot touch. It makes him sound like Oddjob to the Club's Goldfinger – "we abhor violence against our foes, Mr. Bond, but our friend Mr. Meek is less fastidious ...". Isn't he also now free to do the same for us, the increasingly dispossessed traditional support, those who want the truth, however hurtful, rather than Club PR-speak? Will he now do so or are the habits of a lifetime too hard to break? Sadly, I suspect that last question was purely rhetorical.

(First published here, Oct.'95)

UNITED WE SHOULD STAND

'Goal' magazine may like to think it's the authentic voice of the terrace but it was 'FourFourTwo' who first took an in-depth look at the independent supporters movement; the author looked at our contribution, described by one 'Guardian' journalist as a model of modern activism (!).

Given Man. United's recent on and off-field success, the emergence of a critical IMUSA may seem odd, even churlishly ungrateful. Indeed, there are Reds of a Stalinist hue will not countenance a word said against any aspect of MUFC plc – but then, how often that kind turns out to be the comfortably-off, priority season-ticket holder. For the ordinary lads and lasses, bound together by tradition and mutual angst in their Stretford/Scoreboard End strongholds and away ground enclosures, treated as so much turnstile fodder down the years, there was nothing odd about the emergence of the IMUSA: indeed, the only surprise for them was that the inevitable had taken so long to occur.

United did once have an independent fans body of sorts but the Club hierarchy subsumed and emasculated it, ousting the leader in a grubby putsch. Since then, whilst the Club has transformed itself from an underachieving family concern into a Mammon-friendly corporate behemoth, concerned fans have been forced to watch play from the sidelines: impotent and unrepresented, they often feel that they are the victims of certain toxic side-effects produced by the impressive fission that generates the plc powerhouse.

The acutely simple *raison d'être* of the IMUSA has always been to give back to the fans a unified voice. Not that IMUSA ever pretends to speak for all United fans, as their Club-croney critics claim. Whilst no-one is excluded from membership, the short-hand 'true hard-core Reds' bespeaks their target membership: those fans who, despite United's success, remain deeply worried about the direction of the Club and share a sense that they are being marginalized, ignored, priced-out and downgraded. And though many do indeed come from a stereotypical 'traditional supporter' background – young, working-class, vocal males – they have been joined by people from every possible demographic segment, including those normally typecast as being in thrall to the Brave New World of post-Taylor modernization.

IMUSA formed last March after the United-Arsenal match, a three-nil victory marred by an atmosphere-shattering tannoy announcement that bellowed "Sit down or get out" at the jubilant goal-celebrants in the East Stand. The issue of how fans should behave at Old Trafford is but one of a whole raft on the IMUSA agenda, many of which will be familiar to any disgruntled fans at 'modernized' clubs: exorbitant ticket price rises, the abuses of away match allocations, the enforced Club monopoly on

European travel and the apparent dominance of 'business' considerations over football's, all of which can be said to stem from the complete lack of proper fan-Board consultation. But the controversy that raged over the Club's announcement that anyone standing up during play – even in 'traditional' behind-goal areas – could be ejected and banned for life serves as a microcosmic paradigm of the way MUFC and the IMUSA interact. A policy introduced without warning or consultation on the strength of a handful of individual complaints produced outrage amongst the vast majority at the two Ends. 'Traditional' methods of remonstration were used as a first step – a stand-up protest, a leaflet-drop, a public meeting – but the opposition remained 'in the family'. When the Club refused to back down, IMUSA regretfully took the final 'modern' resort of going public; as the leaders are all experienced media operators, they knew how to use both local and national press and radio to further their agenda. After a brief campaign, the Club relented; but most importantly, IMUSA followed-up with some aftermath reconciliation by submitting detailed proposals on how to avoid problems with fans behaviour at Old Trafford and by offering their full support in order to achieve the Club's and fans' common goal of satisfying customer demands.

Certainly, IMUSA's work with the media has produced very visible results: high name-recognition, good agenda-exposure, an IMUSA quote being a sine qua non of any serious United story. But modernity is the key to everything with IMUSA, which is ironic given that they stand for many traditional values. They employ everyday techniques such as computerizing, Internetting, members' opinions polling methodology, running a media-monitoring and supplying unit and so on; but they have also eschewed old-hat oppositionism. By using the language of their quarry – the Board and plc shareholders – in their arguments and documents, they seek to demonstrate that they are not the 'enemy within' but a potentially invaluable conduit to improve producer-consumer relations. Their current glossy proposal brochure, ready for the November AGM, would not look out of place in any corporate HQ. As even quondam arch-critic David Meek concedes "they're a smart and articulate lot": whatever anger and resentment Reds have felt in the past, business is business and IMUSA knows that co-operative solutions are all that a plc wants to hear. That's what they offer – for now at least. Because as chairman Chris Robinson, not a man known to make idle promises, states clearly, "we're not going away: this is no short-term pressure group."

(First published in 'FourFourTwo', Nov. 95)

You can join the IMUSA by writing to: IMUSA (Membership), PO Box 69, Stretford, Manchester M32 0UZ.

. . . news from Muraroa Reds. © EMJ 1995

Part Three:

'WE HATE CITY, SCOUSE, LEEDS SCUM ...'

1. 'Oh Manchester – is full of shit?' (partly ...)
2. Away In A Dustbin
3. For Blue Eyes Only
4. Forward With Franny?
5. City's Band-Aid: Do They Know Where Wembley Is?
6. Anfield: Bottle-Free Zone
7. Jailbaiting
8. '... and Leeds and Leeds and Leeds'
9. Shooting Up The League
10. Criminal Justice
11. Kits Out For The Lads
12. Why Does Everyone Hate Blackburn Rovers?

"OH, MANCHESTER – IS FULL OF SHIT?" (partly ...)

No Mancunian fanzine reader could have missed Peter Hargreaves's heartfelt letter that was printed all over the shop last year. To paraphrase crudely, his message was that Blues and Reds should lay off each other a bit and create some inter-Mancunian harmony; less virulent bitterness from them, no more '18 Years' from us. He recalled the old days when Mancunians would support the other team in big matches or Finals and enjoins us to get that spirit back. The underlying suggestion was that Manchester is entirely wonderful and that for the greater glory of Mancunium, we should welcome the prospect of two successful clubs and even celebrate it.

There's two levels to this. The obvious one concerns the call for mutual support, the plea from every Red's dad down the ages. Perhaps in the 1950s such generosity of spirit was quite nice, in a cute all-Scousers-together kind of way. But however desirable a return to such a utopian state of affairs might be – and that's highly debatable – too much venom has flowed under the bridge since then to make it anything more than an old man's pipe dream. As long as City remain inferior, they will continue to be consumed by Magooism; should they ever reach our level of achievement again, both Blues and Reds will be too fired up with aggressive competitiveness to make a 'truce' possible.

It's the second, deeper level to Hargreaves's argument that needs bringing out to the surface. He has sympathy for City simply because they're fellow Mancunians; because he clearly believes Manchester is flawless, this Manc-ness alone makes City deserving of our secondary support. Basically, this is another expression of what you could, oddly, term 'Mancunian nationalism' which was much in evidence last season during the highly boring Mancunians v. Rest debate. There are clearly plenty of provincial zealots who believe that just about anything that emanates from Manchester is de facto superior. They are often prepared to champion stuff that, if it came from another city, they wouldn't give a second glance. And it seems that even in these tribal times, there are those who welcome a City win against any 'outsiders' because at least it's a victory for Manchester.

The 'Manchester is perfect' school are a bit like the raving feminist who'll support any sister-in-strife, whether justified or not, just because she's a woman or, more aptly, like the bigoted nationalist who thinks everything English is automatically superior to anything foreign. Imagine Manchester was an independent state; would we really expect all its citizens simply to act as one big brotherhood and support a one-party state just because they're all Mancunians? Of course not; we're all individuals of different classes, tastes and opinions who, as in any other state, would divide into groups and struggle democraticaliy for our particular interest.

So, as a Mancunian who does believe Manchester is Britain's greatest city in all the things that matter – footie, beer, telly, music and women – I still say this to Hargreaves and his ilk. This city is just as full of shit, knobheads and rubbish as any other (except Liverpool of course). The best of Manchester is the best in Britain no question – but there's plenty in this city that's crap and that doesn't deserve support just because it's Mancunian. You should go for stuff because it's good, not because it's come from some particular location. I'm proud of United, Boddies, Corrie, the Roses and Steve Coogan in the first place because they're Mancunians but I love them because they're the best. Take That, Bernard Manning and City may be Mancunian but they're also shite and no amount of pride in our city can get round that.

So when it comes down to the nub of Hargreaves's mentality, I'll stick my neck out and admit the logical conclusion to all this. I'd rather have a night out with a Red from, say, Cornwall than a Bluenose from Manchester. Frankly, I don't think that City fans are all loveable fellow Mancunians ready to be our best mates, united in local brotherhood. Throughout my life I've honestly found Blue Mancunians to be 'different' to Red ones; they have tended to be more bigoted, less open-minded and far more screwed up with petty provincialism and small-minded bitterness than Reds I've known. All my best mates have turned out to be Reds not because I've purposely avoided Blues but because I've just thought they were sounder blokes. To, me, City as a club represents the shit side of Manchester and United represent the best. I don't hate City as such, certainly not compared to the likes of Leeds or the Dirties; I just feel a mix of disdain and pity for them. They're just another shitty aspect of our city like the madness in Moss Side, Little & Large, the Oldham BNP bastards and Mick Hucknall. Manchester is Wonderful – but don't forget the crap, especially when it's got a Brother shirt on.

(Sept. 94)

AWAY IN A DUSTBIN

Nobody can deny that the 5-0 was the greatest derby victory in living memory – it's a mathematical fact. But for sheer drama and back-from-the-brink heroics, the post-Galatasaray trip to Maine Road in the autumn of '93 would take some beating, as Red Issue contributor TONY J. remembers.

There are away games and there are away games. There are cold mid-week nights at the Goldstone Ground watching poorly-contested 0-0 draws when the rain drips from your nose and the conversation inevitably turns to a discussion on what you are actually doing there in the first place. There are trips across the Pennines to Helland Road, where you know the sadly inadequate and deliberately orchestrated lack of away tickets leave you vastly outnumbered and in real danger of being separated from your vital organs. There are boring, tedious away games, mildly amusing away games and 'well, it was just about worth the trip' away games, but if you're a very lucky bunny indeed every so often there is a mind-blowing, heart shuddering, 'wouldn't have missed it for the world' away game. Bertie Bluenose: it's the 7th of November 1993 and it's time to come on down and take a bow.

November 7th 1993 was my 30th birthday, a landmark figure I'm sure you would agree, but landmark birthdays don't often also coincide with an away derby at the home of the Permanently Embarrassed. You could say that I was really looking forward to a birthday excursion to Maine Road from the very second I saw the new fixtures in July but that would be a massive understatement. Like a kiddy at Christmas with an advent calendar, every day was meticulously ticked off in mental preparation. The eventual build up to the fixture was somewhat spoiled by United's untimely departure from the European Cup at the hands of the botty-stabbing brethren of Istanbul. Every Red knew those desperate and listless creatures over in the no-go area would obviously be out to try and take the piss but let's face it, that's a bit like Claudia Schiffer gaining a couple of pounds and being barracked about her figure by Nora Batty.

I quite often drive to distant away games myself but a trip on the coach with the North Manchester Supporters Club usually gets the nod for slightly closer encounters. The added incentive of being able to consume copious amounts of birthday alcohol did figure slightly in the final choice on a mode of transport. After perhaps a little too long in the local hostelries in Failsworth and perhaps a few too many birthday beers, we eventually set off for the short trip into The Land of the Shadow People. The expected sound of the local Huns rejoicing in our Turkish defeat greeted our arrival at the ground. 'Two nil up and f*cked it up, Galatasary' sang the unusually witty Bitters as we left the coach. As usual it was a minor failure by United and not a significant victory by their own team that managed to stimulate the vocal chords of what must be the saddest set of supporters in the whole division.

For the completely uninitiated who have never had the dubious pleasure of a trip to Moss Side to watch United in action, I will briefly try and describe the phenomenon of the Bluenose at home. The mere mention of anything United leaves the local bumpkins frothing at the mouth and displaying the sort of facial contortions usually associated with a child being force-fed a particularly nasty medicine. Random acts of cowardly violence on lone United fans are to be expected but this aggression miraculously disappears when the numbers are somewhat more equal. We are not particularly welcome in this footballing backwater and to be honest the feeling is completely mutual. I personally cannot even muster the ability to feel sorry for City and their continual bad fortune. They remind me of a persistent wasp in summer; no great particular threat but can be very annoying at times and need a good swatting now and then. The only consolation for most of us on a trip to Maine Road is the fact that United are highly unlikely actually to lose there and most visits culminate in the speedy acquisition of three points.

On arrival at our seats I was slightly miffed to discover that my own little corner of the North Stand came fully equipped with its own partially obscured view thanks to a large section of concrete. To be perfectly honest, I could have probably watched the game in a reasonable manner from the seat I had been given but I'm sure you will agree that an opportunity to harangue and argue with people stupid enough to volunteer as City stewards should not be given up lightly. I demanded a new seat for myself and my brother and was surprised when the steward said that we should follow him and he would see what he could do. After some minor consultation with colleagues, he told us to sit in the empty block of seats that actually formed the segregated portion between the two sets of fans. I therefore ended up being the nearest United fan to the pungent and disgusting odour of Bluenose emanating from the other side of the stand. By the time the game kicked off, we had been joined by about twenty other Reds and quickly became front-line targets for the amazingly juvenile abuse that was aimed across the remaining empty seats by the monkeys to our right.

Football is, as we all know, a cliché-users dream and the old 'game of two halves' ditty finally came of age on this murky afternoon. Although United did not actually play particularly badly, the half-time whistle found us nursing a 2-0 deficit and some slightly bruised egos. Thanks to the big Irish lamp-post Quinn and his ability to guide headers past stationary United defenders, my birthday wasn't going particularly to plan. Those two badly-defended goals had created half-time scenes not seen at Maine Road since, well, since the last time they were in front in a derby. Being the United fan nearest the massed ranks of grinning, pointing, screaming Berties had quickly lost its appeal, so a trip to the toilet seemed a logical move. On the whole United fans are a pretty positive bunch and the consensus of opinion in the queue for the sadly inadequate toilet facilities was that we were still in with a shout but being a blind optimist does not feature particularly highly on my personal list of recognised attributes. The painful knot resident in my stomach before every derby match is a fair testament to that fact. Therefore, despite the general positive demeanour of my fellow Reds, I headed back to my seat in no-man's-land with an amazing sense of foreboding. Silly, silly, silly me!

What followed in the second half of that game has since variously been described as: brilliant, amazing, cruel, heartless, and just plain unbelievable. With a measured and calculated stride that totally belied any justified urge to panic, United played possibly the best forty five minutes of football seen on a British ground all season. The signs for the Hun were ominous from the start. With all pretence of attacking football stricken from the agenda in a desperate and spineless attempt to hang on to their fortunate lead, City could not have prepared their forthcoming demise any better. With concentration at levels strong enough to give nuclear physicists a headache, United's patient probing and prodding of the Bitter defences began.

Before too long, a breakthrough. Always alert to an opening, Cantona kept one eye on the linesman and one eye on being just goal-side of the City defence. The not-always-so-alert Michel Vonk carefully used his large square head to guide a speculative Bruce header right into the path of the lurking Frenchman. A few Gallic strides and a pin-point shot later, 2-1. More careful approach play and a couple of missed chances even had me thinking there must be something in the game for us. Cometh the hour, cometh the man: Ryan Giggs finally entered the fray and quickly took up the call to arms. Cantona, whose orchestration of United's cause was described on TV as 'looking like he's got a baton in his hand', once again found himself coming from deep to try and create an opening. Two or three close quarter passes skirted the City penalty area and the ball fell to our newly-arrived prodigy on the edge of the box. With an awareness and cool that defies description, a first time pass with virtually his first touch was threaded through the hapless City defence and met at the far post by our mercurial French band leader: 2-2.

I don't need to describe the feelings to any of you because you've all been there yourself. Suffice to say that the only person that escaped a rather un-macho passionate embrace was the policeman to my immediate right – and even that prospect briefly crossed my mind. Red voices strong and loud, filled with passion and hope now drowned the cursing Bitter infidels, whose taunting of us had been replaced by the sad and predictable anger now directed at their own bench.

The videotape of the final goal is solely responsible for the shoddy state of the rewind button on my remote control. Sharpe, with his back to goal flicks a cheeky pass off the inside of his left foot to Irwin. Mr Reliable knocks the ball towards the touch line and races onto it to deliver the perfect cross. A crowd of players lunge goalwards in a desperate attempt to make contact, with the ball just escaping their eager attentions. With the sort of timing that Rolex can only dream of, Keane arrives at the far post and steers the ball just inside the upright: 2-3, good night and God bless. The next few minutes are a total blank for me personally. I know from the video that Keane peels away in celebration towards the Main Stand and blows a kiss before shouting 'I Love You'. He loves us? If he'd have been within five feet of me at the time he'd have been pregnant two months later. My vocabulary sadly cannot sufficiently cope with the task of describing not only my own emotions but also the faces of the those recently grinning morons to my right. Being the nearest United fan to the Blue Goons had now taken on a completely new meaning and only the speedy intervention of the local constabulary stopped me swallow-diving off the top of my seat down the empty rows of space below me to what surely would have been a very messy end.

God, if such a person exists, has got to be a United fan. How else can you explain any divine power building up the hopes of the Great Unwashed to almost fever pitch, before letting them suffer such a devastating, cruel, crushing and decisive defeat. Ultimately it was actually very, very funny indeed. Forget the cards and the presents, forget the party and the phone calls, United gave me exactly what I'd been hoping for all year as a derby day birthday boy and the cake had its own little icing on. 'City is your name, City is your name: two nil up and f*cked it up, City is your name'

(by TONY J., first published here)

DRASTIC!
BERTIE MAGOO
THE BITTER BLUE
BLUE
WELL READERS, LOOKING AT THIS SCRIPT IT APPEARS THAT I'M TO APPEAR IN A BOOK BY RICHARD KURT....
BLUE
..WELL I REFUSE TO BE BITTER JUST TO APPEASE YOU UNITED FANS.....
READERS
UNITED
RESPONSE
LETS TRY BERTIES PATIENCE...
5-0
SHRUG
SHITE
+3=8-0
PRETEND
0-8
YAWN
FRANNY LEE IS A BAG OF HOT AIR AND THE NEW KIPPAX STAND IS A FUCKIN' PILE OF PANTS
HMMM
HMMM
BITE YER TONGUE!
DOUBLE WHAMMY
19 YEARS AND COUNTING
GO ON... YOU KNOW IT MAKES SENSE..
BRING BACK SWALES!
MMM MMMMM...
HMM...
PICCADILLY PHONE-IN...
RIGHT READERS LETS SORT OUT SOME PROPER BAIT.....
HOW ABOUT A SHITE MANAGER AN OVERWEIGHT, OVERPRICED RUSSIAN WHO'S HAD ONE GOOD INTERNATIONAL.... FOR 'GEORGIA'...
3 PRE-SEASON THRASHINGS AGAINST SHIT SCOTTISH OPPOSITION.
AND A PROMISE OF AN END OF SEASON RELEGATION DOG FIGHT...
GO ON BERTIE!
BITTER BAIT
REEL REEL
BITTER
GULP!
REEL HIM IN!
REEL! REEL!
REEL! REEL!
YOU'RE NOT FROM MANCHESTER!
BELL'S BETTER THAN BEST!
KINKLADZE'S 10 TIMES BETTER THAN CANTONA!

FOR BLUE EYES ONLY

The prolonged 'Swales Out' campaign at Maine Road kept us all amused for several months during our Double season as Bluenose hordes actually kept us off the back pages once or twice by virtue of their increasingly desperate agit-prop activities. Our mole leaked us the following top secret bulletin (or perhaps I made it up ...)

Kings of The Kippax Direct Action Wing: Summary For January 94.

DEC 28: At home to Southampton.

We had asked for chants of 'Swales Out, Franny In' every five minutes for 30 seconds throughout the first half. Unfortunately too many of our lads can't afford watches or even tell the time so this was not a total success. The post-match demo was cancelled after our placards were nicked by the local Doddies to make roaches.

JAN 3: At home to Ipswich.

Match abandoned after 39 minutes by southern bastard referee. Obviously a United fan as he doesn't come from Manchester. Demo organized spontaneously to protest against the victimization of City by the, er, winter weather. We note that this never happens at Old Trafford and must be a result of the Rag-loving media's conspiracy against us.

JAN 8: FA Cup weekend.

Protest against the failure to win the Cup for 25 years. We know this is a result of draw-fixing by the FA who want to see United at Wembley and us out which is why they make us play at the toughest of grounds, like The Shay and Gay Meadow ..... er .... our direct action cells will be organized to invade the pitch at the first sign of impending defeats thus forcing replays until we finally get through to the next round. NB: Will volunteers please wear United scarves during these excursions so that we can spread conspiracy theories for weeks in our fanzines.

NEXT SKY LIVE MATCH:

Prevent City game being shown by dropping keks and mooning at cameras. We never win Sky games, presumably because the lads can't handle the thought of being watched by more than 20,000 people. United forced this Sky deal on the rest of us for this very reason.

NEXT WEDNESDAY:

Pre-match demo and march on Town Hall to protest against expected 2p rise in price of Turkish Delight which collectively will cost us a fortune at the next derby game. Future demos to be organized about media portrayal of Moss Side, United always being on Match of the Day and the lack of City star pictures in 'Shoot'.

FINALLY:

It has been suggested that we are devaluing the fan protest as a weapon by having one every bloody week for whatever reason takes our fancy; critics say it's a pathetic attempt to appear important and take some attention away from Stretford United because aggro is the only way to get City on the telly. Nothing could be further from the truth nor is it the case that we are total paranoid obsessives about United, desperate to get the glamorous Reds to pay some attention to us – of that there can be no doubt.

PS: Members shouldn't miss the joint workshop in Bootle with the Liverpool Action Group entitled 'How To Win Public Support By Continual Self-Pitying Whinging'. Don't bring your cars however.

FORWARD WITH FRANNY!

(Jan. 94)

FORWARD WITH FRANNY?

Come on. Be honest. Deep, deep down inside, underneath the jokey exterior that makes cracks about bog rolls and gleefully sings '19 Years', there lurks a fear that the Franny hype is true. That a new era has begun. That wads of dosh will roll into Maine Road. That on a wave of relief and celebration, the Bittermen will emerge from their Greater Moss Side shacks to watch a team that might start playing football and even attracting decent players. What if, horror of horrors, City became ... a good team!?

If you're a teenager, none of this might strike a chord, since you've never known the Blues to be anything but a complete and utter joke. You might think that the club's only reason for existence is to provide something for us Reds to piss ourselves laughing at and even feel pity for; for approaching two decades, City have been the beggars in the footballing street.

However, if you're an old bastard like me, heading towards the abyss of 30, you'll understand this deep fear. You'll remember that for most of the 70s, City could legitimately claim to be the best team in Manchester. Ha! Look at those words! Have you ever seen 'City' and 'best' in the same sentence before? But it was true. Even in 1976 when we managed to finish higher than City for once, they still found the time to hammer us 4-0, a result that scarred me for years. I had no time to loathe the Scousers or the Sheepmen; I was too busy trying to survive in a playground full of mini-Bittermen.

So I take the threat of a resurgent Franny-led City very very seriously indeed; I have no wish to return to childhood trauma, ta very much. Of course, it is more than likely that all this hype will explode in the Blues faces, showering Manchester with pustules of Bitterness. Can any Blue have confidence that City will know how to spend the bog roll millions, if they eventually materialize, at all effectively? Can we look forward to a procession of Steve Daleys marching into Moss Side and becoming as shite as the current side? Perhaps Lee will prove to be such an incorrigible businessman type that he'll be as tight-fisted as Alan Sugar or even end up seeing City as his personal cash cow (like someone we all know, hey kids?)

Anyway, all I want to make clear is that one shouldn't be ashamed to admit to feeling just a tinge apprehensive, to fearing that we might not be able to sing '25 Years and won f**k all' one day. Maybe it would be a good thing if both City and Liverpool got their act together; trophies are more fun when whipped from under the noses of deadly rivals. It's hard to feel hostile about bloody Norwich farmers or Brummie Villains as we were expected to do in '93 isn't it? So I can handle a new improved City but only as long as United remain one step ahead at all times. Alex, I'm relying on you. I don't want to go back to feeling eight years old again. I'd look daft on a mini-Chopper.

(Feb. 94)

Heading for the Maria: this man was caught standing up in K-Stand

CITY'S BAND-AID: "Do They Know Where Wembley Is?"

Street-cred obsessed Bluenoses were chuffed to bits when a City-supporting 'supergroup' (sic) got together to perform for them before a recent Arsenal game. We're not sure what the purpose of this little gig-ette was; perhaps they were raising funds for City's Coca-Cola trip to Wembley, now sadly cancelled after the Eagles' four-goal swoop. Whatever, the Magoos revelled in the musicbiz glamour of it all, despite the effect it had on the team's performance – they got stuffed 3-1.

But what a motley crew they assembled as proof of City's new footie/music cross-over pedigree. Johnny Marr, once a guitar God, now as barren as City's trophy cupboard having produced only one decent record since he wrecked the Smiths – and that was with the help of a Red, Barney Sumner. Oasis, whose predictable collection of three-chord tricks mixed with stolen riffs and melodies palls into insignificance compared with the Roses' meisterworks, as anyone who's been near a guitar in their lives will testify. And finally, King of sad himself, Billy 'The Cult' Duffy, a ham-fisted string-strangler of no fixed talent whose hilarious group thinks it's Led Zep born again. Pardon me far not being orgasmically impressed.

Contrast this with the Dream Team line-up that would constitute a United supergroup – not that they would ever be such Establishment cock-suckers as to play at the behest of tacky football club chairmen like Lee and Edwards. Barney and Co. from New Order on keyboards, samplers and programmers; Morrissey doing the lyrics; The Roses' rhythm section; John Squire on lead guitar; Shaun Ryder and lan Brown sharing vocal duties; Bez doing his maracas bit and supplying the 'stuff', with Take That as roadies to procure the teen jailbait for the lads. There you go – a world-beating group with not a Hucknall in sight. In the meantime, we recommend Bluenoses buy a copy of "Que Sera, Sera" – it's been so long since they've had the chance to sing it, they must have forgotten how it goes by now ...

(Feb. 95)

ANFIELD: BOTTLE-FREE ZONE

Are they on some sort of recycling kick at Loonypool these days? Once upon a time in the days of Smith, Yeats and the original scallies, you could at least count on the Dirties to show a bit of fight, a bit of bottle. However, in recent years, it seems anyone stopping at Anfield is required to chuck any bottle they might have straight into the bin marked 'no longer necessary.' So used had they become to easy title wins against poor opposition that they've forgotten what it's like to be up against it. Check out the sort of behavioural patterns those bred over there have been exhibiting:

KENNY DALGLISH

Takes over a winning team and wins a spawny double in a year when Everton were the best team in Britain. Team outfought two years later by a bunch of hod-carriers at Wembley. Later couldn't take the heat against Palace in a semi; left to United to show them how in the Final. First true test comes when ageing team needs rebuilding. Response? Cops out mid-season and leaves mess for sucker Souness to clean up, pleading 'head is going to explode with pressure.' Opts for easy life with Blackburn sugar-daddy. First true test arrives – defending Title and winning in Europe. Response? BOTTLED OUT!

JOHN TOSHACK

Thinks he's so smart he can run Wales and Sociedad at the same time. Imports crappy 3-3-3-1 and promptly gets wasted by a bunch of Vikings. Does he face the music and battle on, Fergie-style? Does he b*ll*cks. Sets record for fastest-ever BOTTLING.

LIVERPOOL IN THE FA CUP

The mighty Bolton and Bristol come up to Anfield to harry, hustle and close down. For Liverpool past, no worries: get down in the dirt and slug it out – This Is Anfield.

Liverpool present: pansy about like schoolies and act like rabbits frozen in headlights as unknown minnows bear down on your goal to end your season. BOTTLED IT!

LIVERPOOL FANS AT HOME

Wait in dark corners for away coaches to arrive. Chuck bricks, CS gas and ammonia at defenceless opponents. When everyone's out in the open and ready to 'discuss matters', disperse rapidly into Murkeydive waste-lands or leg off into Kop. Never stand your ground like you did in 60s and 70s. BOTTLED IT!

LIVERPOOL FANS ABROAD

At Euro finals, pick fights with Italian Family Stand. England away: never be found around when it goes off. Take the chance to get down the shops for some serious robbing. BOTTLED IT!

So: proof that the 90s Liverpool is all gut and no bottle, save the odd Coca-Cola ...

JAILBAITING

Before the first United-Dirties clash of 94/95, the hype-machine was in full effect for the return of one of our favourite Scouse veterans, Jan Molby, who loudly predicted his imminent success. (Where is he now? – on loan to Barnsley.) The chump is an irresistible target whom the author rushed to welcome back ...

Jan Molby is back, our favourite Danish pastry rehabilitated by Roy Evans and a Scouse-friendly media. You might have missed the unintentionally hilarious interview he did the other week with The Observer's Patrick Barclay, whose arse-kissing of Klinsmann the previous week has probably made him every dodgy foreigner's favourite hack. Naturally, there was no mention of women's clothing or gay night-clubs in the piece but the prison sentence could hardly be avoided. Barclay noted that "Molby believes he was guilty of nothing more than a scallyish prank. 'I tried to escape (the police) but there was no dangerous driving.'" And drink? "I'd had a few but it was one of those borderline things." The judge disagreed and gave the assimilated Scouser three months.

Now it's certainly a 'scallyish' thing for a Scouser to do when you bomb through the city streets after boozing in a club being chased by the police – this is an everyday occurrence all over Liverpool. But a prank? In a city plagued by hit-and-runs caused by drunk drivers and joyriders being pursued by the police? I think there's a few bereaved Liverpool mothers who'd argue with that. Anybody who reckons that Molby's misadventure doesn't constitute 'dangerous driving' is probably the type who'd call Heysel a 'regrettable mishap' or Bosnia a 'little local disturbance'.

On being a jailbird, Molby is amusingly melodramatic. Informed that he was being transferred from Kirkham to Preston, he was horrified: "'No way!' I said, 'Grade A category's for murderers' – Preston was a shithole," Molby says, going on to say how harrowing it was. Perhaps we're supposed to think of the Dane as a heroic figure like Clint Eastwood in 'Alcatraz'. The fact is that Preston is a low-level grade B, full of lads in transit for largely unserious offences and hardly some maximum security jail full of serial killers. It may be old and crumbling but it's a picnic compared to the hell-holes that are Merseyside's prisons. Incidentally, Molby admits that the officer who helped him the most when he was inside was a United fanatic. Can you imagine a Scouser doing the same for a United player in Walton? I think not.

Back on current matters, Molby shows that he's soaked up Scouseness to the full by denigrating United players wherever possible. Asked about 'Klinsmania', he implicitly claims to be the best foreign import in Britain. "Who's the most successful import? Cantona, they say, and that makes me think, if we put our medals on the table, it's actually me. I've played in teams .... better than the one he's playing in." Oh dear, oh dear – bitterness outbreak alert. Even if those claims were true – which they aren't of course – is he seriously suggesting that would make him better than King Eric?! Jan, you're not even the best Dane in the Premiership, let alone the best foreigner.

In typical Scouse fashion, he can't even praise one of his own without including a slagging of a Red: "Robbie Fowler is the best young player I've seen in 10 years in England, including Ryan Giggs. He's different, contributes more." Sigh. It's clear that the Rehab of the Flab is complete. Molby is back and exhibiting all the true Scouse tendencies in full: making excuses for criminality, United-baiting and glorifying the self. Let's hope you're playing today, Jan, so we can give you a warm returning welcome.

(Sept. 94)

"... AND LEEDS AND LEEDS AND LEEDS"

One of the sad aspects of the Leeds fan is that, remarkably, he will probably think he's quite a dude. Leeds-dwellers like to imagine themselves as the urban sophisticates of East of the Pennines, inhabiting a mighty imperial city. Pathetically, this 'huge conurbation', which can only support one barely successful football team that's spent most of its life in Division Two, is actually no more than an eye-sore of a shopping centre in the middle of the countryside with a few slums thrown in to contain the lowlife. In reality, it's about as urban as a cow pat – in Leeds, you're never more than five minutes away from a willing local sheep.

The Tykes love their rural mating-grounds; perhaps it reminds them of their roots from which they've only just evolved viz. the cave-dwelling Neanderthal that hunts dark-skinned animals and shags anything with an aperture. See, it sounds familiar doesn't it? Even the favourite Leeds song – 'United (Leeds) United (Leeds)' – with its deep-bass growl of the word 'Leeds' sounds like something from the sound-track of a '50s dinosaur versus primitives movie. Once, having met a Leeds fan who exhibited human characteristics and could even talk in intelligible sentences, I asked him what this chant was supposed to achieve. "It's like in the film Zulu" he enthused, "it's like a native war cry to terrify the opposition." Sadly, he was quite serious. Ironically, in the film the Zulus, despite outnumbering the Brits 50 to 1, retreated; Michael Caine and company were dressed in red, white and black – another familiar scenario ...

Leeds, in short, is *The Land that Time Forgot*. Throughout the '80s, it remained the Capital of Goth, populated by cretinous creatures obsessed by the Bauhaus and Banshees, loping through the streets in back-combed barnets and skin-tight black keks, the laughing stock of the nation's youth culture. In keeping with the city's spirit, the football fans continued to labour under the illusion that skinhead crops, Nazi ideology and mass violent disorder are still a groovy part of '90s terrace culture and that in the post-Hillsboro climate it might still be legitimate to make light of others' real life tragedies. The poor Tykes are stuck in a 1975-timewarp, deluded into believing their team are 'Champions of Europe', holding firm to the '70s hoolie philosophy of outrage and terror and unaware that the rest of the country has decided that Don Revie was a money-grabbing traitorous failure.

The one consolation for the rest of us is that although they are as obsessed as the Dirties and the Bitters about their public image and its perception by others, they are too stupid to work out the consequences of their actions. Even the most moronic of them must regret Ewood '94 – any sharp Scouser could have spotted the PR implications – but they just couldn't help themselves could they? You can take a Tyke out of the jungle but you can't take the jungle out of the Tyke.

(from the author's book 'United We Stood' Oct. 94)

THE LOWEST OF THE LOW

Hate . . . Leeds fans jeer during the minute's silence yesterday Pictures: MARK TATTERSALL *Moron . . . supporter joins in with V-sign*

Soccer's shame as yobs wreck tribute to Sir Matt

By PETER FITTON and BEN BACON

JEERING Leeds yobs shamed soccer yesterday by hijacking a minute's silence for Sir Matt Busby and chanting for their own dead hero.

As other fans paid tribute to Manchester United legend Sir Matt, 1,500 louts sang: "There's only one Don Revie."

They also unfurled a huge banner bearing the name of Revie, the famed Leeds boss of the 1960s and 70s who died five years ago.

The premeditated insult went on despite protests from the louts' own team – and it outraged football's big names.

The scenes, seen live

Continued on Page 11

The Sun gets it right for once

SHOOTING UP THE LEAGUE

Paul Merson was hardly the first so-called 'star' to be exposed as a nose-powderer: Maradona got caught whacking a five-drug cocktail up his nostrils, though after all the coke he'd snorted, it's a wonder that the Nose of God hadn't collapsed long before. With hindsight, we should've guessed it from the start. How else could this self-indulgent, slut-screwing, pill-popping fat dwarf have shed 26 pounds and successfully got into fighting shape for USA 94?

Makes you wonder, looking at the behaviour of some of our domestic characters, what drugs they should have been on all this time. For your own amusement (and, er, on legal advice) the 'perfect users' are left blank so that you can fill in the names of the usual suspects:

CANNABIS

Effects: Slows you right down, man. Impossible to run anywhere. Makes driving hazardous. Makes you crave regular munchies, thus adding to weight problems. Helps remove inhibitions, rendering you susceptible to embarrassing japes in public places. The number one drug in HM Prisons.

PERFECT USER: ____________________

FIFA Sentence: Exile to Loonypool (reserves).

COCAINE

Effects: Ego-boosting delusions; you'll think you're not as crap as you actually are. Manically hypes up your public behaviour; loosens control of your limbs making you prone to waving your arms about in the air wildly, as well as lethally affecting your driving abilities. Removes all sexual self-restraint leading to uncontrolled animal behaviour when confronted by naked flesh e.g. a stripper in an East London pub. Readily available in open prisons.

PERFECT USER: ____________________

FIFA Sentence: wife to get subscription to *News of the World* so she always knows what he's up to of a weekend.

ANGEL DUST

Effects: Pumps you into a frenzy of raging aggression. Makes you think you're the hardest on the block. Can cause user to lash out savagely without provocation but also effects your co-ordination, making you clumsy, lumbering and skill-free. Popular with flashy pimps in 1970s black L.A.

PERFECT USER: ____________________

FIFA Sentence: not yet before panel – Fraud Squad take priority ...

HEROIN

Effects: Halts you suddenly, ruining an otherwise promising career; reduces your mobility to comatose levels and makes you prone to horrendous motor-function disorders e.g. spectacular own goals. Can also increase hair loss. A heroin lifestyle can bring you into the company of the seediest low-life, forcing you to work with disreputable characters whom no-one else will employ.

PERFECT USER: ____________________

FIFA Sentence: he's suffered enough (see above)

SPEED

Effects: Transforms your cardiovascular system, bringing a crimson flush to the face, stamina and pace to your legs and adrenalin surges all over your body. Can lead to ceaseless aggressive mouthing-off and a desire to punch authority figures or anyone else who's in your face. The best of drugs because, like The Who and the Pistols, you can live off it and still be the greatest in the world.

PERFECT USER: ____________________

FIFA Sentence: have to endure World Cup interviews with loathsome Human Slug Tony 'Mate of Big Jack' Francis on ITV.

NEWCIE BROWN ALE

Effects: Not strictly speaking a drug but it's the only buzz Geordies can afford. Makes you believe you're the f*cking Messiah. Totally lacks class, favoured by wearers of Brut. When imbibed, can lead to disastrous haircut decisions. Prolonged usage can give you a whining, pleading voice that makes listeners spew.

PERFECT USER: ____________________

FIFA Sentence: Baseball bats out, lads.

REMEMBER KIDS – JUST SAY YES.

(Aug. 94)

CRIMINAL JUSTICE

"No one looks forward to a trip to the Dell ... the police take a special country bumpkin delight in annoying Northern urbanites." Thus opens the book "United We Stood" and there was good cause to remember that line on New Year's Eve. As the Red Army Expeditionary Force gathered outside 'The Mission' on Archer's Road, the traditional routine got underway viz. Pete Boyle and acolytes standing on tables in the beer garden to lead a hundred or so Reds through the terrace song-book. Within seconds of a rendition of the line " 18 Years and won f*ck all", hayseed-chewing pigs trottered over to hand out warnings about our 'offensive language' – the aforementioned song was sarcastically doctored to run "... and won Donald Duck all." Jokingly, I remarked to a strangely sober Boyle that with police like these about, he'd be lucky to get into the ground: "they probably think a song counts as an offensive weapon."

Sadly, I had underestimated the local constabulary's potential to impersonate total arseholes. Pete was arrested as he tried to get into our end, the police shouting "we've got him!" as they pounced. He was accused of being 'dangerously drunk", held in the cells until 5.15 and forced to sign a caution without legal advice under the threat that he'd be held overnight, thus missing both his train and perhaps his baby's delivery. The irony was that, unlike at Loftus Road where a similar fate had befallen him, Pete was virtually sober, having decided to concentrate on the game rather than drink 'n' sing session.

I mention this episode not just because Pete is a mate but because it illustrates a wider truth; the travelling fan is still treated as a second-class citizen at the mercy of local policing peculiarities and subject more than most to arm-twisting threats of overnight detention, blacklisting and the like. Pete was never charged, nor was any attempt made to 'prove' his alleged drunkenness, for such a trial would have failed. It was simply a case of arbitrary detention under the arbitrary rules of an arbitrary and corrupted system. The sad fact remains that the football fan who chooses to travel away also, de facto, chooses to jettison his rights as a citizen equal under the law. This incident may have been a relatively 'trivial' one but the principle is what counts: we are all seemingly guilty until proved innocent. So much for the Brave New World of post-Taylor football.

Still, there is a happier epilogue to this cautionary tale. Only weeks later, at Carrow Road, one of Boylie's pals fell into the same police-state whirlpool. Arrested, charged and bailed to appear in court months later for trumped-up disorderly drunkenness, he decided to fight it out with the system. The police may have thought he'd submit and plead guilty but, backed by a car-load of witnesses who took days off work to drive down and support him, the pigs found the court up for a bit of bacon-slicing. As witness after witness demonstrated the police's lack of credibility, the court completely acquitted him and awarded him full costs. The lads were stunned but delighted, naturally: fans' victories over the forces of 'law and order' remain rarities. But perhaps the verdict reflected a wider trend in society – after a decade in which the police have so often been exposed as deceitful manipulators or perjurers in major cases, the trickle-down effect has resulted in 'ordinary' people being given the benefit of the doubt by both magistrates and juries. No longer can a policeman expect to be believed without independent corroboration, thank God. Football fans about to suffer the consequences of the appalling Criminal Justice Act have one straw to cling to: there are increasingly courts out there who know the score regarding our helmet-headed friends. The police will doubtless continue to act as a law unto themselves, treating all away fans as easy arrests 'n' convictions but if you and your allies take them all the way, you might still get a result. As John might have sung, "I fought the law – and the law lost."

(First partially published Feb. 95)

KITS OUT FOR THE LADS

There are three unavoidables in life: death, taxes and media outcries when United release a new kit. You would think that people would grow tired of whingeing every year about the latest Umbro abortion but it seems the appetite for counterfeit outrage is still unsatisfied. The latest Tesco-bag sartorial disaster has, of course, topped the lot in the cynicism stakes. Not only was it released after Christmas, when many would have received 'obsolete' kits as prezzies, but its design bears only the most tangential relationship to United's history. So when an Independent On Sunday journo phoned me up for my opinion on this and other merchandising matters, he was no doubt expecting to hear me parrot the usual anti-Edwards / Freeman diatribe.

"So, what's your view on this cynical exploitation then?" he asks.

"Brilliant stuff," I reply. He gasps in horror at the other end of the line.

"Surely you're not condoning this rip-off?" he exclaims frantically.

"Yes. I'd like to see a lot more of it too." I tell him.

As I went on to explain to the hapless hack, I could not give a toss about the entire merchandising operation any more. If you're going to rely on the Super and Mega-store game for a major source of income, you might as well do it properly and screw every penny out of the saddoes who spend three hours at a time in there. Of course it's grossly cynical to bring the kit out after Xmas – but it probably doubled the amount of kit cash United will make this financial quarter. On a pro-rata calculation, merchandising money contributed at least £2.5 million to the Cole fee; if it means we as a Club have more money to spend maintaining our status as the best team, who cares if the souvenir groupies are the ones who are financing this by spending so much on tacky crap?

Of course, I've never worn a club shirt or been inside the Megastore, nor do I have children whining about the new kit's desirability, so this is an easy attitude to take. It's also true that the entire merchandising operation in general is embarrassingly naff and a source of shame; it might even be true, as the last Red Issue suggested, that merchandising considerations will affect team decisions especially where Giggs and Sharpe are concerned. But overall, I feel a warm glow every time I hear some marvellously nasty piece of MUFC product has been a success with the masses. I think of day-trippers shelling out £100,000 in three hours in the Megastore or out-of-town non-attenders getting fully kitted up in their local emporium and feel misanthropically content. Thousands of sad bastards are spending all they've got spare to subsidize our team at no cost, beyond embarrassment, to us – by 'us', I mean the merchandise-subsidized hard-core who keep their money for fanzines, fags and Fosters.

At the end of the day, Brian, how can you have any sympathy for anyone who falls into the following categories of the 'exploited'?:

1) Parents who are so enslaved by their brats that they can't say 'no' to demands for a new kit?

2) Anyone tasteless enough to buy and wear in public the new kit?

3) Anyone so ignorant as to not know that a new kit was coming in January who went out and bought an obsolete kit for Xmas?

4) Oh, sod it – anyone who goes inside the Megastore, full stop.

Funnily enough, the Indie journo mentioned that he was having trouble finding a United supporting parent to go on the record and complain about the kit 'scandal'. That doesn't surprise me. The only people out there complaining are the media and other clubs' fans. Most of us just couldn't care less any more. We live with the embarrassment, of course, which will endure as long as a man so apparently tasteless as Edwards remains in charge. He, as CEO, is responsible for the glitz-shlock bad taste typical of the lower middle class, minor public schoolboy type; this is a man who thinks names like "Europa Suite" and "Premier Lounge" are "classy", a man who thinks introducing Fred the Red the day after we retained the title was tasteful timing. So, if we're always going to be continually blushing about the latest exploits of the Commercial Department, at least let's have the consolation of knowing that we're making a packet out of it. Let's face it: anyone paying £40 for that new shirt and wearing it deserves to have their wallet bled dry.

(January 1995)

WHY DOES EVERYONE HATE BLACKBURN ROVERS?

Propaganda is always better when it's disguised rather than obvious, as Goebbels once noted; given the opportunity by 'The Game' to write an 'objective' piece about our backward cousins, the author wheedles in as much anti-Rover ammo as possible ...

It wasn't so long ago that Kenny Dalglish, the Rovers manager, could claim that the entire country was behind his boys as they sought to topple Man. United from the English throne. Not any more, it seems: after the valiant failure in 93/94, Rovers are at last in the driving seat but the nation's applause is muted to say the least. However delighted neutrals might be to see the Old Trafford Reds pipped to the post, it's getting harder these days to find anyone with a good word for Jack Walker's battling Lancastrians. Just what have football fans got against them?

Talk to any supporter following a lower division side and you can bet they'll mention money first. "Not only are they trying to buy the Title" says John Watson, a veteran Stoke fan, "but they're doing it with money that they've got from a rich fat-cat, not from cash that genuine supporters have stumped up." There's a feeling amongst fans of clubs that are of similar size to Rovers that there's something 'illegitimate' in being financed in such a way. Burnley's Scott Turrow, who like most Clarets "hates Rovers even more than United", touches on the underlying politics of Rovers' fortunate position: "Our gates, and our potential support, have always been greater than theirs but we have to rely on what our community can afford to give to our Club. Rovers get themselves a sugar daddy and they're made for life. That Club doesn't really belong to the local people – it's Jack Walker's private plaything. They don't really deserve that success."

Envy isn't perhaps the most attractive of emotions and it's harsh to blame Rovers supporters for their luck in being beneficiaries of Walker's munificence. Nevertheless, other Premiership fans have a different angle on the money question – they argue that they're all suffering from the transfer and wage inflation caused by Walker's spending. Dave Williams down at Norwich doesn't begrudge Chris Sutton for his choice of Ewood Park but is concerned about the long-term Walker Effect : "You can argue that it's good to have new money injected into the game from outside but in fact it's a recipe for rampant inflation – it's just more money chasing the same amount of goods. Blackburn's wage-scales force the rest of us to compete and it's the supporters who have to pay the players at the end of the day." With admirable selflessness, considering his club got a £5 million windfall from the Sutton deal, he cites the transfer as the perfect example of Blackburn's prime responsibility for the new transfer madness. "In one stroke, the value of every player in the League doubled as a result of that over-valuation. It's all very well saying that it was the result of supply and demand in a free market but that market has been grotesquely distorted by the Walker money influx and the fact that Rovers can always afford to raise the highest bids."

So much for the world of soccer finance: what about the team and its football? There is no doubt that they are a formidable unit who have set the highest standards of success even without such injured players as Batty and Gallacher – their points and goals record since late 1993 speaks for itself in volumes. Should they win the title, how could it be argued that they wouldn't be worthy Champions? Man. United fans might contend that Rovers' three defeats against the Reds will suffice to question Rovers' supremacy – like Liverpool in the early 80s, Rovers are a points-amassing machine, clocking them up relentlessly against lowly-placed opposition whilst not necessarily winning the big, tabletop clashes. Nevertheless. that is the nature of League football: the team with the most points are supposedly 'the best', whatever the strength of United fans' moral arguments.

Rather, it is the nature and style of Rovers' football that causes resentment and which might yet deny them the mantle of 'true' Champions, whatever that might mean. The gentlemen of the press have no doubts on this one – the consensus of the qualities at least is that Blackburn are too rigid, workmanlike. predictable and, well, boring to garner the accolades that were United's for two seasons past. Typical of the media's sniffy view of Rovers was the response to Blackburn's 3-0 win at Wimbledon before Christmas: "dreadful"; "tedious"; "a cure for insomnia"; "you fear for Rovers in Europe next season". The well-worn lines and channels of Blackburn's 4-4-2 machine might win the points but is never going to excite the neutral as much as, say, Man. United's same-scoreline win against the Wombles last February.

Perhaps, like the great Liverpool and Leeds sides before them, Blackburn will eventually flower into something more beautiful once the initial trophies have been won. For the time being, however, it looks like their fate is to suffer the sort of sneering commentary that Leeds received in the late 60s, like this in the fanzine 'U.W.S.': "The phrase 'form follows function' could've been designed for Rovers – no thrills, routine and workmanlike. The football lacks style, the club charisma; potential Champions should be offering more."

For Rovers-haters, the litany continues further; Kenny Dalglish doesn't exactly endear himself to observers with his grudging, taciturn public persona whilst poor crowds at Ewood for games such as Trelleborgs and

Newcastle cause rival fans to yell 'Part-timers!' and 'Where's yer atmosphere' at every opportunity. More serious critics predict doom for Rovers in any future Champions League and worry about the effect on the English game as a whole should Blackburn get scalped. But the editor of Rovers 'zine 'Loadsamoney' is happy enough in the face of such criticism. "I can understand how the rapid timescale of our rise has annoyed a few people but that's their problem. We've got a good team with class players and we're England's top scorers – I'm quite content to pay good money every week to see this team, believe me! Yes, we might have a few bandwagon-jumpers here but most are like me, twenty years of watching Rovers and now enjoying the time of our lives. Some people hate us but that's because we're top of the league, so that's to be expected. And in the hate-stakes, we're still a long way behind Man. United."

Maybe it's as simple as that: success breeds hatred. United and Rovers have more in common than they think, perhaps ...

(First published in 'The Game', Feb. 95)

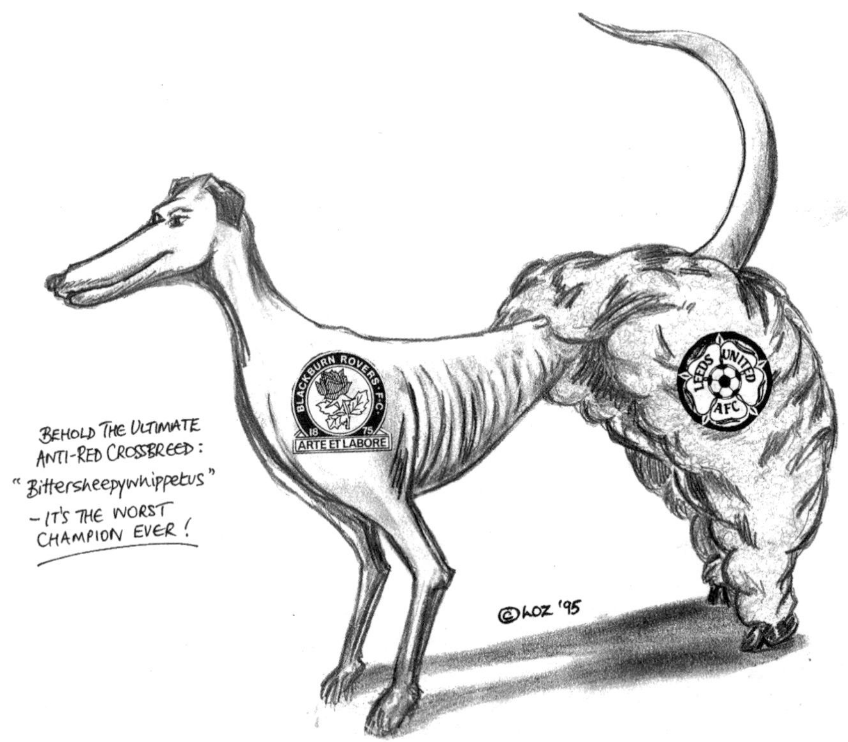

The Best Of THE DAILY SPURT 1993-96

FEATURING SOARAWAY REPORTS ON:

Ralphie Bribery Scandal – Maine Road Plague – Engelbert Cantona – Debbie Does Moss Side – City Bomb squad – Richard Littledick – Mystic Slut – Nazi Sperm Horror – Jeanette Trollope – Crimewatch – Local News Updates . . .

. . . and much much more

THE DAILY SPURT – gives it to you straight up the arse

BLUENOSE CRIMEWATCH

THERE WAS little surprise when the Manchester Evening News revealed that Ballbarings-busting futures dealer Nick Leedson is a Man City fan. At the moment, Leedson is of course, like many City fans, in the nick – is that why City can't even draw 20,000 to important Cup ties? – but his colleagues in Singapore have revealed the cause of his downfall.

"Sadly, Nick got heavily into the City futures market. We warned him that he was letting his heart rule his head but he wouldn't listen," said an insider.

Leedson is alleged to have invested over £1 billion on a stock exchange sporting index – he was the only trader in the Eastern hemisphere who took up an option that City would finish the season in the top six. There are even worse losses to come that the new owners of Ballbarings must handle: said our source, "Nick even stuck several hundred million on City winning a trophy before the decade is out. The local traders don't know much about football but even they knew that this was a sure-fire loser. They couldn't get in on it fast enough. Ballbarings will be paying out on this forever.

Manchester City have hotly denied that Leedson had anything to do with the Steve Daley deal or the employment of Malcolm Allison. Meanwhile, Leedson refuses to concede he might have made a mistake on the City trophy futures deal. "We're a big club", he burbled from his Frankfurt cell, "and will win several trophies in the next few years, mark my words." Lawyers handling Leedson's case are considering an insanity plea as the best defence.

MANCHESTER HEALTH UPDATE

THE NEWS in a recent survey that Manchester is the fourth most depressed place on earth has come as a surprise to most of its inhabitants, particularly Reds who've had the time of their lives for the past couple of years.

The Daily Spurt can explain it for proud Mancunians, however. The percentage of Mancs who are depressed or who have mental disorders is 24.8%. We suggest that figure is probably the exact percentage of Mancs who are Bluenoses. As any City fan after the 8-0 Double must be virtually suicidal and given that most Blues are clearly mentally defective, we think the mystery of miserable Manchester is solved.

THE JEANETTE TROLLOPE COLUMN

The First Lady of Chorlton Street: 'The Columnist Who Gives It You Straight'

BOB BLEEDIN' WILSON! Arncha sick of the sight of him?! Who does he think he is, going on the box every week telling us all we should be supporting Blackburn in

Europe? The only support they'll get from me is if the boring sods bugger off to Europe and stay there. Do we want the frogs and wops to think we're even MORE boring than the Germans? It's bad enough having John bloody Major 'batting for Britain' without having David Batty 'Hoofing It For England'. Tell you what, we should appeal to UEFA to have Harford and his Lanky Donkeys banned from Europe 'cos they're doing more harm to our reputation than Scousers.

FARTIN' MARTIN EDWARDS! Public school smoothie-chops you might be my love but you were in danger of making me LOSE MY LUNCH when you got your onions out and started weeping about United fans shelling out too much for Wembley trips. Well call me a cynical old pussy but what chutzpah from the boy wonder – after announcing yet another kit change!! Try this for size you naughty young pup: you keep your poxy coach refund and we'll keep the £60 a throw you'd want for the strip. Bleedin' United Clothing – they're doing more lines than Jimmy Corkhill.

RUBBER-JOHNNY GILES!! Cos let's face it, his slaggings of Monsieur Cantona stink of rancid poo don't they? And didn't he look a knob when Eric replied to his wicked words by signing up again for the Reds. Sweetie, we know rejection can be cruel and that you've never got over Sir Matt dumping you in the Elland Road dung heap but be grateful for all the sheep you've enjoyed as a result. Get a life man! No-one likes a sourpuss – and I should know darling!

'FUNNYMAN' EDDIE LARGE!! Do us all a favour Eddie and don't go back on telly to boast about your love of City. Your perm gives the kids nightmares, you're even more disgustingly obese than the boiler-with-the-bell behind the goal at Maine Road and your attempts at anti-Red wit only remind us all why the Beeb axed your show. If you approached me as a prospective punter, you're so yukky even I would give you the bum's rush from my rum bush. City's most famous fan!! It's very sad really isn't it boys?

JEANETTE'S HUNK OF THE MONTH: Eric Cantona – you can stroke your balls near my goalmouth any day mon ami! Ryan Giggs – come up and probe these openings! Coley – is it true, big boy?!

More deranged columnist rantings every day in the Spurt, Sun, Mirror, Mail .....

UNITED IN 'NO DISASTERS' SHOCK HORROR!

Normal week outrages football

MANCHESTER UNITED rocked the football world to its foundations this week by failing to make any cock-ups, insult its fans, sell any star players or stage a tabloid bust-up. Gutted hacks cried into their expense-account whiskies as ashen-faced United officials admitted, "It's true: all we've done this week is a spot of training and played a couple of matches ."

SHOCK

FANS were in shock as they turned to the back pages and found other clubs in the headlines.

"What is going on at our Club?" asked one fan outside the Megastore. "I didn't send back my season ticket for this. I demand the Board gets back to its job of screwing up United now."

Blame was being squarely laid at the door of manager Alex Ferguson, who is alleged to have told United staff, "Can we please stop f*cking about and start being a football club again?

LAUNDRETTE

JOURNALISTS were stunned when they even failed to get either Mr. Edwards or Mr. Launders to say something stupidly insulting to the fans. "I can't believe it," wailed *The Spurt's* Lunchtime O'Booze, "Usually you only have to put a mike in front of either of them to get their feet in their mouths. They're simply not doing their job."

COCK UP

HARASSED United officials promised they'd do their best to get the Club back on course. "I'm sure this competence is only temporary. Give us a week to get back in touch with Inter Milan about Eric and to bring David May back in the team and normal cock-up service will be resumed," said a spokesman.

UNITED ANNOUNCE SUCCESSOR TO INTER-TOTO CUP

THROUGH THE KINDNESS of their hearts, the imaginative geniuses who look after Old Trafford's finances have come up with a top tournament to replace the unloved Inter-Toto Cup. "We're sure that United fans will rush to support the team over the next two summers as we play the Milanese for the 'Inter-Transfer Trophy'" claimed Ken Meritless. "The trophy itself is a glittering silver bust of Paul Ince and the medals feature portraits of Steve Kutner and Denis Roach in tribute to their efforts this summer."

SHEEP-SHAGGERS

UNITED are sure that their loyal sheep *(surely 'fans'? – Ed.)* will happily fork out thousands of their hard-earned pounds in order to help Italy's richest club meet United's price. "It's another commercial first for us," beamed Ken, "asking Reds to pay the fee for the loss of their terrace hero. We think this competition will run and run: perhaps we could make another trophy for when we flog Eric."

BUGGER OFF

RESPONDING to criticisms from supporters' spokesman J. Flaxman, Meritless shouted: "As we said on 'Newsnight', if they don't like it, they can go and watch the Reserves. Our Chairman's market research says we've got 70 million fans throughout the cosmos so we haven't got time to listen to those who actually go to the matches. Anyway, if I were you, I'd make the most of these Inter games: after our great Summer Sale, it's the only European football we're likely to see here for quite a while."

NEW MAY CONTRACT DETAILS REVEALED

IN THE WAKE of Eric Cantona's mould-breaking "pay-as-you-play" contract deal, United have taken the opportunity to apply the same principles to other players, starting off with David May .

"We've made Davey's a little different to Eric's" announced finance chief Robbin' Launderer. "Basically, he'll start each week on £5,000. If we're forced to play him, for example when every other defender in the Club has a broken leg, then he goes down to £4,000. Every shit header then costs him £500, every bottled or botched tackle £250 and every goal he's to blame for a grand. I suppose it's not so much 'pay-as-you-play' but 'fork-out-as-you-f*ck-up'."

May's agent, B. Magoo, was reported to be less than happy with the deal: "David will be f*cking bankrupt by Christmas." The Club have denied that Lee Sharpe and Brian McClair are to be offered similar terms ...

DAILY SPURT EXPOSÉ EXCLUSIVE!

KRAUTS IN NAZI SPUNK SHOCK!

EUROPEAN football's leading Kraut crackshots were accused today by Professor Batson D. Seeling of being the products of dastardly S.S. genetic experiments.

"I'm afraid they exhibit all the behavioural signs associated with Hitler's chosen brigades," claimed the controversial academic, "which leads me to conclude that they were fertilised in a test tube using frozen sperm saved from the Third Reich."

MASTER RACE

The Prof's theory is that Martin Boorman and company escaped to Paraguay in 1945 loaded up with SS spunk so they could recreate the master race at some future date. "We are now beginning to see these creatures emerging in the world of sport," says Seeling, "but their disgusting unsportsmanlike behaviour is fortunately giving them away."

DIRTY CHEATS

The footballers are joined on the Prof's hit-list by notorious cheats Boom-Boom Beck's and drug fiend Katarina Knob-Krabbs. "All these square-headed bastards play sport as dirtily as the SS fought the war," fumes the boffin. "Instead of fighting fair and playing footie in the trenches at Christmas like the Jerries used to, these monsters shoot Tommies in the back and dive for penalties. Prof. Seeling points to Uwe Rizzla's sending-off at Highbury and Klitmann's dive against United as continued proof of their evil genetic make-up and claims that Rizzla's ridiculous 85-style footie haircut with long fluffy bits at the back is evidence that he's only just arrived from the South American Nazi colonies. 'The Third Reich is attempting to seize control of the Premiership," seethes Seeling "and they've even brought some allies from former Axis power Romania to help their sinister infiltration."

BRAZIL NUTS

The Prof., who reckons Klitmann's test-tube father was a U-boat captain thus explaining the constant emergency dives, argues that we should only allow foreigners who fought with us in the war to play in Britain – like the French and Danes. "After all, you don't want to be cheering on someone whose forebears might have wiped out your family do you?" The Prof later denied he'd been watching Gregory Peck's 'Boys from Brazil' whilst on mescaline again.

DAILY SPURT NEWS KIOSK UPDATE

CANED BUT ABLE

TORY politician and best selling 'writer' Jeffrey Archole looks set to bounce back from his recent troubles over Anglia TV share-dealing, according to friends.

Said one admirer: "Just examine his track record. A minor public schoolboy made good, he's faced allegations of liaisons with unsavoury women and insider dealing yet come through with his marriage and finances intact. What an inspiration to all Conservatives he is."

Asked what career such a profile was fit for, the Archole fan had no hesitation in replying: "Why, he's obviously got all the attributes needed to be the next Chief Exec. of MUFC, hasn't he?"

CHAINS OF OFFICE

THE DESELECTION by Liverpool Labourites of the Deputy Mayor, Petrona Lash-me-down-tightly, who was due to become Mayoress, has caused outrage and consternation on Merseyside.

Party members turfed out the mother-of-three councillor after the Liverpool Echo revealed her history of convictions that have since been 'spent'; it was felt that the public wouldn't accept a Mayoress with her 'interesting' past.

A bemused local expressed sadness at her removal from the Toxteth ward: "Yes, she's got convictions for brothel keeping and deception but I'd have thought that would make her a perfect representative for our city ..."

BLUES BEHIND BARS

THE WELSH Mountain Zoo at Colwyn Bay that made local headlines after it named two penguins Giggsy and Hughesy has come under attack from City fans demanding equal respect for their club.

The zoo, which receives many Manc visitors and renamed the penguins as they were the most popular attraction, has promised to make amends to bitter Blues.

A curator told us: "We've got two candidates for new names. One's a red-coated hyena with an incredible hypersonic yap that reduces everyone to hysterics: the other's a gorilla who goes berserk with the slightest provocation, whom nobody in his cage likes." Alan Balls-up and Terry 'Mickey' Phelup are said to feel 'honoured'.

THE DAILY SPURT CHARITY APPEAL

WE ASKED the stars of the football world if they could help those less fortunate than themselves this New Year by donating any unused Christmas presents to us for resale – all those items that they didn't like or didn't want. Here's what they generously gave to your caring, soaraway Spurt.

TERRY PHELAN: Muzzle, metal collar and one dangerous animal licence. Said Terry, "I don't understand why I was sent these – I ain't got a dog ..."

JAN MOBY-DICK: Inflatable doll (female). Donated unused. Jan reckons he was prepared to use it but it only had one orifice which was no good to him (?) For some reason the doll has had a moustache and perm wig attached.

TONY ADAMS: Hilarious novelty do-it-yourself breathalyser kit in the shape of a fire extinguisher! Nozzle flavoured with Four Seasons pizza taste; when over the limit, plays theme tune from 'The Bill'.

KAREN BRADYBRUNCH: The Bum City supremo got a new Giggsy poster for Xmas so she's let us have her old one although it's rather crumpled and smells a bit fishy.

LEE CHAPMAN: A video of the love classic 'Un Homme et Une Femme'.

OSSIE ARDILES: Interest-free Xmas loan-bonus from Spurs for 'scouting duties in Lithuania' (Held in Jersey Central Bank in used fivers).

JIMMY 'BROTHER OF FARTIN' EDWARDS: Complete set of My Little Soldier toy guns.

MARTIN EDWARDS: Granada's 'Best of World in Action 1980' video set.

ROBBIE FOWLER: Face mirror.

We would like to thank all those concerned who sent us their donations and special thanks to the reader who sent in a video called 'How to hit the f**king target' for us to give to Brian McClair next Christmas.

DAILY SPURT EXCLUSIVE!!

DEBBIE'S A PREMIER STRIKER – "I SCORED EVERY TIME!"

FORGET the News of the Screws and Martin '£100' Edwards; we've found a girl who's played on every pitch going! Buxom blonde bombshell DEBBIE MULLER's been on intimate terms with all the Premier Big Boys and she's confessed all to the Daily Spurt. She's no stranger to Manchester either; Debbie is a well known 38/24/36 figure in Moss Side as pouting Deb explains.

"Yes, I met Alan Ballsup at a top hotel in the city (Vera's B&B in Ardwick) and it was lust at first sight. We toasted each other with tumblers of bitter and fell onto the bed. He was such a gentle, considerate lover although he had a bit of trouble finding the centre of my goalmouth if you know what I mean! He said it was a common problem where he worked so I guided him in myself."

GOING DOWN

But it all ended in tears and confusion for Debbie. "One night I plucked up the courage and asked him if he would go down on me but he just went wild. He shouted that he was not going down under any circumstances. His voice was screeching like a stuck pig's and I was really scared. I tried to make him feel better and said it was OK, I had every confidence in his abilities but he just burst into tears and wailed that 'Franny never tells me owt like that!' Well, I assumed he meant he had another woman so I had to give him the boot. He just laughed strangely and said I wouldn't be the first to do that to him. It was all very bizarre."

BLOW MY WHISTLE

Things began to look up for luscious Debs when Francis LeeOnePen took her under his wing, plying her with wine, exotic holidays and naughty awaydays in his Roller. Their sex life was perfect and her loving pudding-head satisfied all her oral needs – but she began to have her doubts when things took a slightly perverted tone. "He just loved diving down on me but it was getting a bit out of hand – he was down there all the time. I got a bit worried when he asked me to blow a whistle every time he went down on me and shout 'Penalty'. It seemed to turn him on alright but I thought it was a bit odd to say the least. Then one day he asked me if I'd like to meet his horses and I knew it was time to get out!"

IN THE BOX

It wasn't long before Debbie was introduced to the boys in the dressing room and started administering post-match relief.

"Terry Phelup – what a wild boy he was. Loved his S&M, especially when I put him in a dog collar and dragged him around the bedroom on a lead. I had to call him 'Rover' and let him sniff my bum. But I had to dump him after he bit a huge chunk out of my arse. But he was a real animal in bed."

Which was more than could be said for the other City boys:

"Some of the lads who played up front were useless though; didn't have a clue where to go or what to put it in. They'd stick it frantically wherever they could – anywhere but the target! I complained about being left frustrated and unsatisfied but I think they'd been told that before."

RED HOT PUS

Deb's a regular on the Kippax now and says she feels at home with the other City girls; "We all have similar standards". She's only strayed once when she was taken to a Scouse Reunion and fixed up with a young Liverpudlian called Robbie. "It was a nightmare. They asked me to do a favour for a physically disadvantaged lad but nothing could have prepared me for what lurched through the bedroom door. I ran off screaming – put me off sex for at least a week. The smell of pus was overwhelming."

Debbie's now embarking on a career as an actress: "I've got a part with a film company called Electric Blues; I think it's something to do with City with that name." Well, there's lot of knobs in it, whatever.

'BIZARRE' – SPURT SHOWBIZ NEWS

CANTONA KUNG-FU: EVIL EASY-LISTENING INFLUENCE TO BLAME?

THOSE who've been looking for karate-kick precedents in football's history should instead direct their attentions to the hellish Las Vegas world of M.O.R. easy-listening. As the 'National Enquirer' reports (see caption), none other than greasy singing lothario Engelbert Humperdinck was the instigator of this latest trend in performer/spectator aggro. And our sources tell us that Eric had long since fallen under the crooner's spell by the time he performed his feet-flying homage to E.H. at Selhurst Park.

"It all began when Eric heard the Hump's late 60s classic 'Les Bicyclettes de Belsize"' claims our insider. "Eric was fascinated by the unique half-French lyric sung in an appalling Hollywood accent – and the song's whimsical images of England convinced Eric to cross the Channel."

Needless to say, the bouffanted balladeer's hits have continued to form the sound-track to Cantona's life. When his troubles at Leeds developed, the 1967 smash 'Please Release Me' was never off Eric's turn-table; then when Tykes turned against him

Engelbert: The night I broke a fan's ribs with a single blow

Legendary ladies' man Engelbert Humperdinck is quick to admit he's a lover, not a fighter — but that doesn't mean he can't protect himself in a pinch.

A longtime karate student, the 58-year-old singer reveals he put his self-defense lessons to good use when he was attacked onstage in Las Vegas one night.

"I was reaching down to shake hands with people in the audience when this guy took hold of my little finger — and broke it! Then he jumped onstage and grabbed my hair," he recalled in a candid interview.

"I reacted instinctively the way I'd been taught in karate. I hit him once and he was back in the audience, lying on his back with broken ribs.

"I don't mention this to show I'm some kind of hard guy.

"Quite the opposite. I'm an entertainer who sings songs of romance. I'm in the game of love, not fighting."

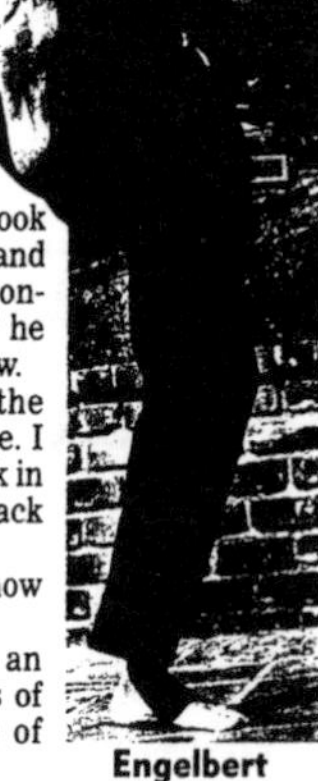
Engelbert

after his move, Eric consoled himself with the sympathetic words of 1969's 'Am I That Easy To Forget?' And now, no doubt, with his future in the balance after his Humperdink impersonation went horribly wrong, Engelbert's 1970 classics 'The Last Waltz' and 'Too Beautiful To Last' are never far from Eric's hi-fi stack.

All this may be as ridiculous as claiming that the Dublin Riot was an imitation of, and directly caused by, Eric's little outburst. But it didn't stop both the Mail and Sun making the same pathetic accusation did it? Frankly, these days you'll find more truth and honesty in the National Enquirer – or even the Weekly World News – than you will in any cheap Fleet Street product, apart from your soaraway Spurt of course. Meanwhile, rock on Engelbert.

PRINCESS ROAD PLAGUE PANIC

CITIZENS in the heart of Moss Side are cowering in terror tonight as the scourge of pneumonic plague threatens their lives. The deadly disease which broke out in India recently is alleged to be infesting the area, thanks to the influx of unwitting carriers coming back from seeing their families on the subcontinent.

Locals are particularly concerned that the sheer amount of rats, rubbish and unwashed down and outs in the area are only making matters worse. "The symptoms are just frightening" says Dr. Jaballah, the deli owner who doubles as the community health practitioner. "Victims start frothing at the mouth, their voices become manically strangulated and they lose control of their brain and motor functions, making them prone to disastrous physical and intellectual cock-ups."

The doctor is also puzzled by the changes in skin colour that can occur: "Their entire bodies can turn green, which seems to be bizarrely triggered by watching United on TV, but their noses remain bright blue. I just don't understand it."

The local football club refused to comment on reports that their manager and one of their full backs have been taken into quarantine; their spokesman bubbled briefly at the nose before muttering strange incantations that included "five-one" and "we're a big club".

DAILY SPURT UNDERCOVER REPORT EXPOSES MORE SLEAZE:

"YES, I TOOK BRIBES TOO" – RALPHIE MILNE

FOLLOWING the shocking pictures of Bruce Grobelaar allegedly taking back-handers to lose games, United star of the 80s Ralphie Milne has stepped forward bravely to admit his own dreadful sins.

B*LL*CKS

Speaking from a makeshift shelter in a wood outside Bristol, the former Red winger owned up to the lot. "They used to call me the new George Best" remembers Ralph "and United had their eye on me from the minute I broke into the team at Ashton Gate. Alex used to tell me not to play too outstandingly well in case someone else spotted me before he'd tied up the deal."

BOOZE

Milne got his dream move but he'd scarcely had time to warm his boots when sinister forces took hold of his life.

"I fell in with a bad crowd at Old Trafford" moaned Milne "who spent all their time taking me round the drinking clubs of Manchester and putting all their beers on my tab. I was too young to resist and before I knew it, I owed local gangster bar-owners thousands."

WIGGY

Milne was at his most vulnerable when he was approached by a shady local character, "a small-time businessman with an amazing Shredded Wheat wig" recalls Ralph. "He promised he'd pay off my debts if I played crap for the Reds. I was on a sliding scale, with money being paid on the basis of which Old Trafford stand my crosses landed in."

Ralph became less than popular with the OT crowds who never realised that a devastatingly brilliant footballer lay just below the surface. Ironically, the businessman never paid up and Ralphie was forced to flee the city. "He phoned me one night and told me he wasn't going to pay. Apparently all his cash was tied up in instalment payments for something he'd bought in Wolverhampton in 1979 – so I was finished."

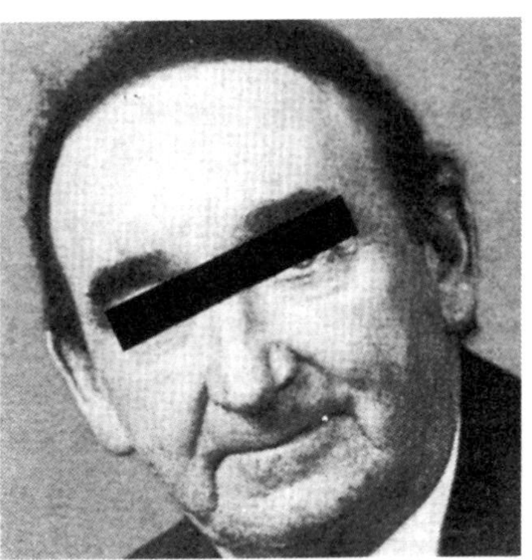

The sinister Mr. Wiggy

CHOCCY

Milne's remarkable story has prompted others to come forward – Paddy Roche, Tommy Jackson and Tom Connell have all announced that they too were potential superstars ruined by temptation. No current stars have yet been implicated although leading figures in the butcher's trade speak darkly of 'enormous pie-related debts.'

COMING SOON FROM THE DAILY SCUM:

FANTASY FOOTBALL LEAGUE FOR SAD BASTARDS

IT'S THE NEW craze that's swept the nation, kids! Are you a sad, lonely supporter of a second-rate team with no star players and no chance of beating Man. United? Then Fantasy Football is for you. Retreat into your own make-believe world of fairies, dragons and Man City trophies and create your own little universe where, just for once, you might be on the winning side.

Fantasy Football: the talk of the pubs as fans of inferior teams desperately try to avoid the reality of their utter crapness.

Fantasy Football: brought to you by every bandwaggoning rag in the land – especially popular in Leeds and Moss Side.

FANTASY FOOTBALL – WHERE IT CAN BE 5-1 EVERY DAY!!

CHURCH NEWS

NEW BISHOP OF DURHAM IN "I BELIEVE IN CITY" SHOCK

MICHAEL TURNBOLLOCKS, who succeeds controversial David Jenkins, astonished his congregation yesterday when he declared his belief in the Second Coming.

"Yes, I truly believe the Championship will return to Maine Road after all these years in the wilderness. I have been praying for years in the church of St. Francis, patron saint of shit-paper, for this miracle."

The Bishop went on to express his deeply-held convictions that Elvis will be the next President, that aliens will be the Christmas Number One and that Michel Vonk will one day be Player of the Year.

The outgoing Bishop Jenkins commented from York Minster: "I might have upset some people over the years with my own outrageous comments but at least I've never been such a cock as to predict a Title for City. Some miracles are out of even God's range."

YOUR TV HIGHLIGHT TONIGHT:

"SNATCH OF THE DAY" BBC1 10.50pm – featuring highlights from the Louis Edwards Memorial Trophy

Panel regulars for tonight are:

TERRY VENABLES who'll be talking about the use of Italian restauranteurs and dodgy holding companies in modern football.

TREVOR BROOKING on how to enjoy life with the Sports Council by claiming £114,000 in expenses between you.

ALAN HANSEN will explain the tips he's picked up from working alongside cheating Scouse divers all his footballing life.

Tonight's presenter is Frank Bough – not that he's involved in anything dodgy; he just fancies watching grown men squirm under pressure ...

YOUR DAILY SPURT STARS WITH MYSTIC SLUT

WE IN the astrology world have all been thrown into confusion by the shift in the zodiac that was widely reported recently. However, we discovered a completely new star sign that governs all United fans whenever they were born. To check if this new sign really works, we look back on the predictions we made in January 1995 following the conjunction of Cantona and Selhurst.

– You will hear the tune 'Where's Yer Mama Gone' everywhere with the word 'Cantona' strangely inserted.

– Dark gruesome strangers from over the Pennines will laugh in your face and shout 'told you so.'

– Emissaries from every city in Europe with a football club will be reported in the Boothstown area on mysterious missions.

– A Welshman will return to try to claim the Crown of Old Trafford.

– The men they call the Rovers will pass several moons trying desperately to claim they were not 'gifted' the title of Kings.

– The Beast from Thornton Heath will be severely mauled, court or no court.

– You will rediscover your love of the cup they call 'UEFA'

– You might wish your only source of power was not just that gained from coal mined in Newcastle.

– You will find yourself drinking in strange foreign towns on Tuesdays not Wednesdays.

One prediction is certain to come true – you will wish that Geminis could keep their bloody temper ...

LOCAL NEWS ROUND-UP

OFF THE RAILS:

LIVERPOOL City leaders, who last week announced plans on Look North to build a new lo-cost tram system, have been explaining how they can manage to construct an entire network for 30% of the price of Manchester's Metrolink.

"We intend to use the best of Liverpool's local skills and ingenuity to achieve these superb savings" explained Councillor Bazza Sinbad. "We're going over to Manchester to f*ckin' nick theirs."

KRAPSHOT KRAUT:

Following the shocking assault rifle attack on President Clinton's White House, the FBI have arrived in Moss Side to hunt suspects. "We think we could be dealing with a psychotically deranged Bluenose here," said agent Jed McBurger. "The assailant took over twenty shots from close range but missed with every one."

CAUTIOUS CAUCUSES

Security forces in Vladivaskaz have been puzzled by the media fuss made over their supply of thousands of troops for the visit of Liverpool to the war-zone. "What did you expect?" asked Boris Marshallov. "We have learned that when Scousers are around, it's best to have as many police on duty as possible."

TODAY IN HISTORY

With Uwe Rosler and those 'hilarious' German bomber T-shirts in mind, we look back to a Daily Spurt edition from World War Two.

THE DAILY SPURT **March 12th 1941**

FIFTH COLUMNISTS SUSPECTED AFTER RAID ON OLD TRAFFORD

AIR RAID wardens at the scene of the football stadium's devastation suspected local traitors were responsible for guiding Hitler's death bombers to target Old Trafford.

"Local residents report shifty-looking, possibly drugged characters hanging about just before the raiders arrived. They were carrying torches which we think were to illuminate the target zone" said an ARP sergeant.

"They wore strange insignia, presumably the symbols of some sick sect – shirts with "6-1, 1926" on the front in blue letters".

Officials are puzzled as to the location of this group, although sightings have been reported in some south Manchester ghettos. They refused to confirm or deny local reports that the collaborators were heard shouting "Bomb the Rags! Bomb the Rags!" during the raid; police wouldn't elaborate on the possible meaning of leaflets they left behind headed "Who's got the biggest pitch now, then?"

THE RICHARD LITTLEDICK COLUMN – Irritant Of The Year

AS READERS of my old column in The Sun will know, I'm very fond of these mock-dialogues that fill an entire page and allow me to insult people under the cloak of satire. Imagine, if you will, the final meeting when the FA gave Vegetables the England job and read on. Don't forget to tune into my Sky News show and help me ensure the viewers are more numerous than the guests ...

F.A.: We want you Terry. You're a Southerner, which frankly we prefer and you have a proud record of not actually winning any trophies in England thus continuing a noble national managers' tradition. Above all, the press want to have your babies and it would be nice for us not to be called senile incompetents for once. We're just a bit concerned about these allegations in the F.T. about your business affairs. Put our minds at rest, Terry, so we can whitewash the whole thing over for you.

TEL· Cor blimey Guv, my old man's a con man, strike a light etc etc ... You gents just tell me what's givin' you grief an' I'll get on the dog and sort it pronto, so 'elp me.

F.A: Well, these 'advisors' of yours, they're not exactly saints are they? We're sure you're totally kosher, but is your good reputation being sullied by association ...

TEL: Say no more. Know what you mean. No trouble at all, guv: I'll drop all my advisors a.s.a.p., even the ones who've got no actual convictions. Then you'll feel safer knowing that I'm takin' care of all financial business personally.

F.A: Er, right, I'm sure we all feel our money is safe in your hands ...

TEL: And it's gonna be even safer. I've arranged for all F.A. funds to be transferred to a special Offshore Taxsaver account in Jersey, secret number, no names, no pack drill, knowwhorrimean?

F.A: Very enterprising I'm sure but ...

TEL: And then there's investments gents, your money's not workin' for you, gotta speculate to accumulate dontcha? I've found you lucky people a luvverly little number to get yourselves into, a class West End joint called Scribbles – it's gonna be the Club of the Nineties.

(LAWYER: What, like Palace were the team of the Eighties then?

TEL: Shut it, you slag.

LAWYER: And where's my six grand fee then?

TEL: Cheque's in the post, straight up.)

F.A: Do you think we could get on to footballing matters now?

TEL: All in good time, me old china, just thought of another nice little earner – financial schemes sponsored by England players! Can't fail, just picture it, the Bryan Robson Pension Plan, Tony Adams Motor Insurance Scheme, the Gascoigne Hospital Fees Fund, blimey the possibilities are endless ...

F.A: I suspect it is time to end this meeting now; I'm sure Terry has eased any concerns we might have had about any fiscal shenanigans, so let's make it official and pop down the Savoy for a spot of lunch.

TEL: Right you are, squire, I'll take us down in my run-around, I can do you a sweet deal on a reconditioned Merc y'know ....

Part Four:

LOOK BACK IN RANCOUR

1. Getting Hammered
2. Cup Final Memories – 1979
3. Cup Final Memories – 1985
4. Anfield '92
5. Smart But Casual
6. Touched By The Hand Of God

GETTING HAMMERED

The last League game of 94/95 took us to Upton Park, instantly conjuring up memories of Title deciders in '67 and '92 – but the pugilistic atmosphere of the day was more 1975 than anything. In "The Red Army Years", the author looks back to the 'Battle of Upton Park', printed in 'Red Issue' as an appetizer for that fateful afternoon.

Nothing enrages more than the media cliché. Tired and emotional hacks who can't be bothered finding the news, the truth or even an original metaphor all too easily dip their gin-soaked hands into the bag of Media Myths, ready to slap on the page and fill another column-inch. Reds know them all too well; the witty sporting Koppite ready with a song and a smile; the eccentric surrealist humourists that are the 'true Mancs' on the Kippax; and West Ham as a welcoming, family club, preaching the best traditions of the game in a luvverly East End atmosphere. Stick Trevor Brooking on the Beeb, refer to Saint Bobby Moore every other sentence, show a couple of Alan Devonshire goals and, strike a light, West Ham are the nation's fave Cheeky Cockernee Chappies.

Any Red attending virtually any Upton Park game since 1967 will find such myth– making a vomit-inducer of the highest order. Admittedly, we have to hold up our bloodied hands as the instigators of this particular vendetta. In May 1967, United travelled to West Ham seeking, as is well known, a win to clinch the title. What is less celebrated is that this day marked the first full-scale Red Army operation in the capital. Previously, all Northern clubs had trod warily in London, especially in the docklands where Millwall had already established their fearsome reputation. By 1967, United's travelling forces had swelled to such numbers as to breach the banks caution had imposed; a tidal wave of Red swept through Upton Park, including 500 who'd occupied the North Bank. Aggro both inside and outside the stadium resulted in 20 hospitalisations and banner headlines in the Sunday press: "Soccer's Day Of Shame" blazed the News Of the Screws.

What an epochal day May 6th 1967 turned out to be. It was to be the last title winning day for us for 26 years; it kick-started the rise of the Red Army; and for West Ham, it was a day of humiliation never to be allowed again. In particular, the lovable dockers retained a fierce animus against the Reds. Not only had we caused their loss of face, much to the delight of the psychos at the Den, but we would always be seen as the most threatening of all the Northern hoards who would henceforth be descending on the East End. Later of course, the ICF and their hangers-on would export their violent parochialism to away games. Long after Reds had ceased going down to West Ham intent on causing trouble, this 'family' club continued to treat our visits as a declaration of war.

In the run up to our game at Upton Park on October 25th 1975, the 'Hoolie-Hype' was in full effect. The London press was full of blood-curdling predictions mixed with the usual mock-horror sanctimony. The tabloid press in particular bear more responsibility for soccer-related violence than they would ever admit, of course. The undertone of the coverage was clear: the Red Army were 'top of the league' following their exploits in Division Two: they'd shown up London fans at Millwall and Orient; now West Ham could put the Northern yobbos in their place on behalf of the capital. The press are always first in the aftermath of violence to yell 'String em up' or 'Bring back National Service/the birch/summary execution but fail to recognise how much they've helped create an atmosphere of conflict in the first place. So it proved to be this time. The press had set up the fight, provided motivation and then exploited the events to a maximum for the benefit of their circulation figures. Pass the sick bag Alice.

United lost the game 2-1 and were knocked off the top by QPR, but all the headlines were devoted to the riot. Fans arriving in London had been told that the Underground had gone on strike rather than take Reds to West Ham; several hundred had to walk miles to the ground whereupon many found themselves locked out. Moods were not helped when it was learned that the Tube had been running after all. Naturally Reds were attacked on the way to the stadium, outside, inside and on the way back to Euston. During the match itself, Reds on the South Bank were assaulted on three sides, forcing thousands onto the pitch and stopping the game for 20 minutes. Stretchers and police were everywhere. The final tally; 102 injured, 9 in hospital, 38 arrests and 132 evictions.

Predictably the London media had a field day on Sunday. Almost without exception they blamed "United Hooligans" for the disruption. It was lazy journalism at its most catatonic. United had the reputation so why look any deeper? If they'd bothered to do so, they'd have found that 70% of the arrests and 90% of the ejections had been Hammers. Even the local police, who have a tendency in these matters to blame the visitors, had to say "blame does not appear to solely rest with the United fans." Well, thank you PC Plod. The London edition of the Sun, pandering to its audience on Monday, stepped further into the world of the absurd by roaring in its headline 'The day the Terrace Terrors were Hunted and Hammered!' There followed a gleeful account of how West Ham crews had "routed" the Red Army – with not a hint of condemnation. Naturally there was no mention of the fact that the vast majority of Reds had had no intention of kicking-off. The numbers and the terrain made a Red victory unlikely from the start.

Since that day, not a visit to Upton Park has passed without some form of incident, usually taking the form of isolated Reds being waylaid in true scouser style by a pack of East Enders. Such episodes rarely reach the pages of the papers, presumably because it contradicts the 'salt of the earth East Enders' image so beloved by the West End-dominated media, just as Koppites still get the benefits of their 1960s image enduring in the minds of the nation. The hammers and their psychopath cousins at Millwall still milk the Second World War vision of blitzed Cockneys, epitomising the strength and decency of working class England. As we all know, in reality Hammers epitomise everything about the modern East End: that it's full of fat, jewellery-laden racist wide-boys who've managed to create one of the ugliest, most hostile environments in urban Europe. As for these much-vaunted 'family values' that West Ham FC is supposedly built on, they actually amount to this; if you're not from the same street, you've an excellent chance of winning a free knife in your belly. Of course, if you're not the same colour then don't bother trying for life insurance. The East End welcomes its coloured brethren with the greatest selection of racist graffiti in Britain, often backed up by a personal welcome from your local BNP activist.

Indeed, of all the disgusting facets of the Hammer, it is the racism that has been the most enduring. Banana sellers can still do good business there on a match day, as Incey recently found out; the Nazi paper 'Bulldog' was freely sold around the ground for a decade. Throughout the late 70s, Hammers could be seen proudly wearing West Ham/NF shirts. But hey, the Hammers don't discriminate; they still hate Jews just as much, as any Spurs fan will tell you. This is presumably some weird throw-back to the days when Oswald Moseley stomped around East London in his puffy jodhpurs. Of course casual racism has always existed at footie grounds, Old Trafford included, but only four clubs have managed to elevate football racism to a sort of art form, to a level where it became almost ineradicable – and West Ham are first among that quartet. For this reason above all, let us hope they return with their jazz-funk CDs, crappy souped-up XR3s and chunky bracelets to their natural home that is the Endsleigh Division One.

(From the author's forthcoming "Red Army Years", pub. summer 96; this extract first published in 'Red Issue' April '95)

CUP FINAL MEMORIES – PART ONE: THE ARSE OF '79

1994/95 ended with yet another Cup Final but one that was almost entirely free of magic – will any Red be writing nostalgically about it in ten year's time? I doubt it. The opponents – and the result – brought to mind the past 'classic' Finals of 1979 and 1985; first, JIM WHITE, author of "Are You Watching Liverpool", recalls the madness of 1979.

There was no prospect of a ticket. It was 1979, my second year at college away from Manchester and, unlike 1977, I hadn't been to enough games to accumulate the tokens. Being 18 and a student I was not exactly Gerry Anderson in the string-pulling department; I was resigned to watching United against Arsenal in the common room bar, dodging the sneers of the rugby followers.

Then on the Friday morning, with less than 28 hours to kick off, I was in a lecture at the end of which a lad stood at the front of the hall and asked if anyone liked football. Thinking he was proposing a kickaround on the Downs or something, I stuck my hand up. I was the only one to do so (well, it was a Middle English lecture).

"You don't," he said, flourishing a bank-note sized piece of thick paper in his hand, "fancy going to the Cup Final do you?"

Did I? I nearly wet myself. It turned out his dad was a director at Middlesbrough and had sent him a ticket. The lad himself, going through a difficult phase, didn't much care for football and wondered if anyone could give the thing a good home. The home I could give it was in the Buckingham Palace class. He didn't even charge me.

The next morning I got the early train to London and travelled north on the tube to Stanmore, to meet two mates I knew were coming down from Manchester. One of them had secured a brace of tickets from a bloke who lived down their road (it was Martin Buchan). So there we were, the luckiest three gits in red, winners of the lottery that is Cup Final ticket allocation, joining the joyful hordes down the Jubilee Line. When it turned out we had belting seats, opposite the royal box and we were only two rows apart, we thought nothing could go wrong.

But for 80 minutes, everything did. It was the most miserable 4,800 seconds football of our football-watching careers. "Sod this for a lark," said the man next to me as events dragged towards their inevitable conclusion; and off he went, assuming Arsenal were going to take the thing 2-0. Immediately into his place sat a big fat man, a pie-eater of some pedigree. I don't know where he came from but we were soon to be introduced.

The man had barely squeezed into his new position, when suddenly, unexpectedly and totally against the run of play, McQueen stuck out a telescopic leg in the Arsenal area and made it 1-2. We leapt up, the fat man and I, and slapped each other on the back. We were still on our feet, roaring more in hope than expectation, as two minutes later McIlroy, stumbling, stuttering, never quite in control, picked his way through the Arsenal defence as if through a minefield. And, we scarcely believed it, with two minutes to go, he equalised.

The fat man and I, we became intimate. We wrapped our arms around each other (mine didn't quite make it round his midriff) and bawled meaningless monosyllables of triumph and relief into each other's faces. We bounced forward in our emotion, tottering over the seat in front of us, tumbling as one and sending the representatives of the Rutland FA, or whoever else it was deemed worthy of a prime spot at the Cup Final, running in spluttering indignation.

Meanwhile, as we tottered, down on the pitch, straight from their kick off, Brady had started to weave towards the United area. Nicholl, though, had fallen asleep; McQueen was still celebrating his goal; and Buchan was still wondering why he had wasted two tickets on the half wit who lived down the road: Brady galloped past them all. He made it to the by-line, crossed and Bailey, practising his victory interview with South African television, let the ball run to Sunderland at the far post.

No haircut has less deserved the prominence Sunderland's fright frizz was about to attain. As he tucked the ball away, his hair, his fancypants grin, his stupid blue collars flapping like birds' wings as he ran off in a victory dash, were all about to become etched on a thousand Red nightmares. The final whistle went almost before he had returned from some sort of sexual congress with Rix by the corner flag.

The fat man and I stood silent, open-mouthed, three rows in front of where we should have been, our wedding plans abandoned. Next to us was a new neighbour. He was an Arsenal fan, a spotty youth, who in his moment of victory did what any self-respecting supporter would do. He stood over us, stricken in our desolation, and waved his hands in a double V-sign at us. He yelled at us, with foam flecking the corners of his mouth, in a screaming fury.

"Why don' you two," he said, "Just fack orf ap norf".

I think it was Nick Hornby.

(by JIM WHITE, from the author's forthcoming "Red Army Years" pub. summer '96)

CUP FINAL MEMORIES – PART TWO: SCOUSEBUSTERS '85

A decade before 1994/95's grim conclusion, the same two teams had met at Wembley in very different circumstances: doesn't part of you miss those days when we were almost always the big match underdogs? Back then, we saw a one-nil to be savoured, not forgotten ...

Scouse-busting is, of course, our speciality – above all when it involves wrecking Double attempts at final hurdles. The Cup win in '85 was so much sweeter than in '83 for this very reason; having buried Liverpool's ambitions in the semi, we now had the glorious opportunity to do the same to Everton at Wembley. Even more satisfying was the fact that we'd been the most barking of underdogs in both confrontations – and this was further topped by the knowledge that we'd beaten eleven players and the officials. In passing, we'd also prevented Everton doing a Euro/domestic treble just as we had done to the Dirties in '77. Short of including Leeds and City on our route to Wembley, it could hardly have been more perfect.

The more thoughtful commentators were billing the game as a classic confrontation of differing philosophies; Everton all hard work, team play and patience against United, the epitome of mercurial unpredictability. As it turned out, we were dragged into the most attritional of battles – World War One come to Wembley. If anything, it made our achievement all the greater; forced into a style of match alien to us, we still managed to beat the Scouse at their own game.

Of course, just two moments from those two hours are stamped indelibly on every Red memory. Policeman-turned-referee Peter Willis had looked uncomfortable all match, like a pig trying his trotter at being human for a day. Willis was already notorious in Manchester for his antics at a City game a week or so before when, according to our backward Blue cousins, he occasioned the most unjustified sending-off in Maine Road history. Obviously, we laughed our heads off at the time but when he fished out his red card to the disbelief of Kevin Moran, Willis ceased to be a figure of fun. For the subsequent half-hour, his was the first name on a thousand hit-lists. It is at least gratifying to think that he will forever be remembered solely as the man who made Wembley's worst-ever decision.

To be charitable, it could be said that he was a victim of a prime piece of Scouse Media Awareness Complex. Peter Reid, upon being felled, did an accomplished impression of Olga Korbut with a wondrous succession of dramatic rolls and pained facial expressions. As soon as he realised that Moran was actually getting his orders, he rose Lazarus-like to his feet in an instant, doing his level best to portray himself as a sorrowful fellow pro. Puke, puke, puke.

Quite gloriously and justly, the only effect of this apparent catastrophe was to mainline a cocktail of purest passion and adrenalin straight into the jugular of both team and fans. It might have been the combined effect of the sun and beer on our vision but Norm and Hughesy seemed to be growing in front of our eyes, forcing an increasingly terrified Everton into retreat. Nothing stirs the spirit quite like patent injustice; no team needs passion like United do. Everything was in place for a *coup de grace*.

Fittingly, Norm was the man to provide it; equally apt that Hughes was the provider. As he dallied on the flank, coming in slightly to survey the prospects, we were mostly, understandably, screaming 'Give it to Strachan!'. Understandable since we were hardly going to be yelling 'Norm – take it yourself and curl an unstoppable shot in from an impossible angle for the goal of the century' were we? Which is precisely what he did. A scarcely credible moment of untrammelled genius had won us the Cup in the most adverse of circumstances. This was glory defined; of all our Cup triumphs, there is a good argument to be made that this was the greatest of them all – and that Norm will always be the King of the Scousebusters.

(May 95)

ANFIELD '92

However bad you felt after Upton Park '95, it was surely as nothing compared to a certain Liverpudlian afternoon three years before; Red Issue's MONSIEUR LEGUME recalls how being banged up was better than having to watch that second goal ...

It was approximately 3.35pm, in the back of a police van behind the Anfield Road End, hands cuffed behind my back, drunk as a lord and feeling pretty sorry for myself, when from behind me came the dulcet tones of Dave being forced somewhat unwillingly into the same predicament. The sound of Dave, drunk and complaining at perceived injustices, has now become legendary amongst those of us who've seen him confront authority from Budapest to Birmingham via Warsaw, never flinching, always in the right, the level of persecution rising with the level of drink. For a second though, as the realisation that we'd both been arrested for what must've been separate incidents hit us, we were momentarily sober in the same way movie stars always manage to gain a clarity of consciousness in the seconds before the bullet finally takes its toll. We looked at each other, pissed our sides, then passed into a drunken semi-comatose state.

How had we got here? Back in August when we were destroying Aston Villa and anticipating the end of the 25-year wait, this day in April had already been looming large. There at the very end of the fixture list were the Club who had done so much to ensure that the wait had been so long. Fantasies were already being spun of how we'd need to go to Anfield needing just a point for the Title; we'd finally be able to rub the noses of the Dirties in it after so many years. This would be our greatest day. Back in August, back in December even, we had every right to expect that this would be our finest hour; it had never even crossed our minds that it would instead turn out to be our worst day since Denis back-heeled us into Division Two.

It had, of course, all started to go wrong on New Year's Day when rumour had it that too much imbibing of Fergie Hogmanay Whisky and/or Brucie Birthday Brandy had allowed QPR a 4-1 win at OT to break the first chink in the United armour. Sure, we'd then gone to the home of the Devil worshippers and stuffed them twice in seven days but the surety of the first half of the season was gone, never to return. We only drew against Notts County, Coventry, Wimbledon, Wednesday and a host of other sides who should have been despatched like errant schoolchildren by any side with designs on calling themselves 'champions'. Then ... then came Easter: make-or-break time and we fouled-up good-style. Hughesy's miss at Kenilworth Road that would have made it 2-0 a minute before half-time haunted me for months; Webb's snail-like departure from the field whilst we were losing at home to Forest was the most treacherous moment I'd ever seen; and Upton Park, well, we all remember Upton Park.

Somehow, though, as we boarded the early coach to Merseydive that Sunday morning, there was still hope in the air. What had seemingly been extinguished in the East End was re-ignited by the flickering flame of optimism that comes with being a United fan. After all, anything less than a win for Leeds who were kicking-off two and a half hours before us at Bramhall Lane and we'd have the chance to get back in the driving seat with a win over the scousers. Typically, the coach radio was playing up but we were still able to hear the news of the Blades' opening goal. Hope springs eternal and suddenly, in Brian Moore's immortal words, the "Title was up for grabs" again. However, by the time we entered 'The Winslow' behind Goodison – home of the legendary two-for-one shorts bar – Leeds were 2-1 up. The pub was showing the Yorkshire game; as pints were downed, bedlam broke out when Sheffield equalized. Again hopes were raised to a state of such nervous disposition that might in other circumstances have made me certifiable. I wasn't even able to watch the game, judging Leeds's progress by the reactions on the faces of fellow Reds. Then, with eight minutes to go, Brian Gayle showed the predatory instinct of a Greaves or Muller and put through his own net. It was all too much for this particular Red. With double vodkas available for the derisory sum of £1.20 a throw, I went to the bar and ordered eight of them. Somewhat bemused, the barmaid asked who they were all for: I pointed at my by now similarly depressed mates and answered "that lot". I lied. If I wasn't going to get the chance to get drunk in celebration a week later, I wasn't just going to drown my sorrows now – I was going to butcher, then bury them in a drunken haze. Sixteen vodkas in less than five minutes on top of the five pints that had already passed my way during the previous fifty minutes was the easiest way of doing it.

After exiting the 'Winslow', the ten minutes it took to cross Stanley Park are not among my proudest moments in eighteen years of United-watching but let the truth be told. The sight of scousers gleefully taking the piss was too much to bear and mention of a certain football-related disaster was made on more than one occasion. My frequent riposte of "at least we don't murder our own" was starting to grate on my compadre's nerves. (The writer omits to mention his highly amusing and shameless encounter with a young Scouse angler here – Ed.)

Of course, by the time I took my seat in Row 2 of the Anfield Road, I was barely able to make out any of the proceedings. My eyes struggled to distinguish between the mass of green and, well, everything else – a kaleidoscope of moving images, none of which I was able to focus on. Rush scoring was the final straw. As the big-nosed one turned to his flock of adoring thieving bastards in the main stand, I muttered "see ya later" to Bert and, with tears in my eyes, clattered my way past everyone in the row for the exit. The next thing I can recall is being sat on a step underneath the stand when a fellow Red urged me to stop feeling sorry for myself, get back inside and urge on the Red-shirted heroes. Now determined to show the scousers true support, I made my way back into the ground via the metal staircase at the corner of the away end. However, I was not to make it back into the ground. The sight of one of our older, female fans being man-handled by a member of the Merseyside Constabulary was like red rag to bull; having aimed a no doubt feeble punch in the copper's direction, I was soon heading for the back of the transit van .... which is where I bumped into Dave.

Walton Lane police station hosted a reunion for the drunk and despondent. By this time I was convinced I had been wrongfully arrested by an over-zealous and spiteful Scouse cop. As the sergeant was booking me and Dave in, we were demanding the duty solicitor; he laughingly replied "you been watching too many episodes of 'The Bill', you have – you've got no fuckin' rights so shut up." We were put in a cell and as others were thrown in with us, we were able to track the progress of the game. United were still one-nil down. Sometime later, as we settled down and sobered up, we heard the voice of another of our mates as he too was checked into the Blue Lamp Hotel. Amazingly, out of the five of us who'd made our way to Anfield, three were now in police custody, all for totally unrelated events. We persuaded a copper to lend our cell one pair of shoes so that we all didn't have to walk through the lake of piss that had formed around the toilet ... it all lent a comic air to a tragic day.

Seven, then eight o'clock came and went; our cell, which had at one stage held nearly ten, now had only me and Dave as occupants and we were wondering if we'd ever get out. Our complaints about our unfair treatment were met with stony silence – obviously our earlier belligerence was now being held against us. Finally, at sometime after eleven, we were offered the opportunity to sign a caution notice and be on our way. This gave Dave one last chance to confront authority: he refused to sign, claiming wrongful arrest. It was yet another comic moment – in exasperation, the sergeant told him that unless he signed, we'd both be charged there and then. This seemed to sober Dave up and we eventually made it back to Manchester in the early hours of Monday.

Looking back, I'm sure it would have been a much worse day if we hadn't been arrested. And of course, Fergie cites the disappointment of that day as one of the driving forces behind the determination not to fuck up the following season. Anfield '92 was one of the lowest points of all our United-watching careers. Still, I'll always look back and wonder how on earth I could partake of five pints and sixteen vodkas in under an hour – a personal drinking feat unsurpassed until September in Moscow ...

(by MONSIEUR LEGUME, first published here.)

SMART BUT CASUAL ...

What footie fans are wearing still matters – witness United We Stand's regular 'House Of Style' musings – but the early 80s was the zenith for terrace style-watchers. In the author's forthcoming pre-Fergie nostalgia book, he casts a jaundiced eye on the first batch of label-groupies.

I once told a Sun-reader that Conrad's 'Heart of Darkness' was a critique of the worst moments of the Sexton years. He didn't believe me but what a perfect title it would've been. The thrills, the passion and the flair of the Doc's team ebbed steadily away leaving us with a barren stodge that was utterly indigestible; no wonder that you so often felt like throwing up after a United game.

How apt that simultaneously on the terraces, the colour was slipping away from the fans. The sea of red and white to which we had become accustomed was being gradually diluted; scarves, hats and the like were going out of fashion as fast as 'Top Trumps'. Not that we should over-emphasize this development; we're only concerned here with the cutting edge in the Strettie, not the acrylic slacks and zip-up bomber jacket brigade in the main stands. But certainly the scarf-twirling banks of red at the End were soon to be a thing of the past and given the tactically hamstrung crap often served up as football in front of us, it seemed appropriate. The reason, however, for this change was that the Perries had arrived.

When you start generalizing in the area of football fashion, you're on dangerous ground of course. How can you apply blanket labels to areas of the ground that can hold up to 15,000 Reds? Not every lad in the mid-80s United Road Paddock was a total nutter; not every person in G-stand is clinically brain dead. But surely it's safe to observe that the 'casual movement' that began to sweep British terraces at the turn of the decade found its greatest support in the north-west and that in Manchester, the most infamous subset were the Perry Boys who soon made their sharply-cut presence felt in the Strettie. No colours as such; excellent Martin Fry haircuts; a plethora of designer labels; above all, an intense, almost Mod-like attention to image, detail and smartness. The contrast with the flared denim/tight T-shirt/excess above-neck hair of the mid-70s norm couldn't be greater – and at least looking back on pix of yourself from the period doesn't make you cringe in horror.

As for the reputation of this new breed, Wellington's phrase about his own troops springs to mind: 'I don't know what they do to the enemy but by God, they frighten the life out of me.' The casual image was one of classic post-modern confusion; clothes speaking of money, style and status in society but probably concealing the heart – and the bloodied

Stanley knife – of the warrior. In fact, a fighter intent on camouflaging his nature from public and police could scarcely have come up with a better disguise. In retrospect, it seems remarkable that the rest of the world took so long in catching up to what had happened.

Rival fans, of course, were totally au fait with every nuance of ever-changing terrace fashion; soon, the footie/fashion cross-over had become yet another arena for tribal dispute. The most celebrated manifestation of this new culture was 'The End' zine, a more talked-about than read publication from Merseyside run by the lumbering plumbers who later became The Farm. The letters pages provided the forum for gangs of fashion-victim footie fans to air their increasingly pathetic rantings about who was wearing the hippest trainers and coolest labels as well as the more predictable 'who duffed up whom' arguments. Rereading back issues only induces tedium so save yourself the bother. The only 'historically significant' issue in it was 'who started Casual?', an honour usually claimed by scousers simply by virtue of repeating 'we wuz first, like' to as many sociologists as possible. As we all know, there's been no new trend out of Liverpool since Merseybeat, unless you count manslaughtering Italians of course.

The casual era lasted, if we're generous, from about '78 till 84/85 whereupon Manchester took a lead in killing it stone dead, north of London anyway. Each club had their own well-defined looks which changed as rapidly as the seasons according to the dictates of 'The Face', 'i-D' *et al*, often resulting in a confusing congruence of style – Mickeys were complaining in '83 that you couldn't tell the Mancs from the scousers until they 'asked you the time'. If it had any significance as an era beyond establishing style as an important permanent feature of the tribal rivalries, it was that it confounded all those journos and academics who were trying to make sense of football violence. It is also probably fair to say that the casual extended the life of football hooliganism well into the 80s; by changing the methodology and image of the fighter, it set back the authorities' attempts to counter aggro by years just at the point when they'd seemed to design an effective strategy.

Whether you view the casual era as a golden age of football culture or a disgraceful aberration, it was certainly richly symbolic; it marked the end of the 70s, the decade that style forgot and heralded the designer label-dominated 80s. And at the home of United, somehow the casual seemed to be the perfect inhabitant of what was becoming 'Cold Trafford'.

(From the author's book "The Red Army Years" to be published summer '96)

TOUCHED BY THE HAND OF GOD

Well, I can't think of any other explanation for something totally fundamental which has changed at United. I hesitate to say it explicitly in case whatever magic has been weaved vanishes upon its discovery but the United of 93/94 have, at last, been blessed by Divine Luck. And the sod of it is that although the results of this heavenly intervention have made me orgasmically ecstatic over this last year, somewhere deep down I miss the old masochist angst that misfortune can bring. What a headcase.

As I write this, the past week has witnessed the following. We won an away match after a crucial pass was played to Giggsy by a corner flag. In a cup draw full of difficult potential ties, we draw the walk-overs at home. Out of the blue, UEFA decide to fix the Euro Cup for the future in such a way that benefits us more than any other team. Then best of all, for the first time in living memory, English fans come out of foreign aggro to be hailed as heroes and saints instead of visigoths and vandals. All this in one week? How fitting for the anniversary of Eric's arrival, for it was November 1992 when, as we can now appreciate, God became a United fan.

For as long as I can remember, United were always spectacularly unlucky; the Fates seemed to conspire against us in the cruellest ways. In fact, it amazes me that we ever managed to win anything even in the Busby years, so determinedly did the Almighty try to screw it up for us. In the old days, we would be allowed to charge gloriously to a dozen semi-finals of FA and Euro Cups before cocking up horrendously; a speciality was beating the best like Benfica before being humiliated by nobodies from Belgrade or chucking away three goal leads from home legs. That era was capped in an almost beautifully miserable way when grinning Destiny allowed City to relegate us at Old Trafford via Denis Law's heel – how immeasurably wretched to be killed by your own King. How typically United.

I started supporting the Reds the day after that match. It seemed to my warped childhood mentality that any team that managed to win anything in such a cosmically hostile environment would truly be champions; the presence of a devil in the club crest struck me as being hugely apt and frankly asking for trouble since God was clearly a Scouser. As Nick Hornby points out in his classic "Fever Pitch", there is an immense grim satisfaction to be gained from feeling that the world is not only against your team but seems to conspire to cause you disaster at every turn. It binds your own kind together; suffering, not success, is what makes the true Red.

I can't write anything about Wembley '76 or '79 because dwelling on those losing goals makes me regress instantly to that greatest teenage trauma; no girl could break a heart like Alan Sunderland or Bobby Stokes did. But the Eighties offered sufficient proof that United were a cursed club to such an extent that every other bugger in the country began to notice. How could they fail to do so when our bad luck gleefully manifested itself in every aspect of our life? Hot new signings would instantly freeze under the baleful glare of the O.T. lights. We would go top on a Saturday; by Wednesday the hospitals would be full of long-term injuries. The F.A. automatically allotted our crucial cup ties to blind officials – and T.V. would helpfully beam these catastrophic events live to a nation that delighted in the rank injustice of it all. 1991/92 was quintessential United; we stuff the Sheep twice, convince everyone we are the best team in the country and yet Fate still contrives to rob us. How outrageously unlucky to lose our best player to meningitis of all things, surely a sign that forces beyond football were at work. How statistically unlikely that four players should separately contract flu on the eve of the QPR game with such morale-shagging consequences. When a few months later Dion Dublin was carted off within weeks of his arrival, I honestly thought that only some sort of Faustian pact with Satan himself would give United the power to overcome this ridiculous quarter-century of cosmic piss-taking. When Eric arrived, my paranoia was such that I considered the possibilities of him being a Leeds agent sent to destroy us from within. There was surely no way that he could actually turn out to be a bargain for I knew it had been decreed many eons ago that all other clubs set secret "United prices" for all their players of treble their worth in an attempt to bankrupt us. Of course I didn't realise that Eric was not as other men and that in fact he had been sent by heaven to remove the curse and to bless us with Divine Luck.

Since then we have all had our moments of Revelation; mine was when he made that cracker for Irwin when his foot virtually kissed the ball to Denis – it's football, Jim, but not as we know it. The Dauphin had arrived – the Prince of Light was illuminating our way to the Holy Grail.

And so it has come to pass that in the twelve months since his coming, the Force has been with us. The few minor reverses we have had were caused by us, not by Fate. Everything goes our way. Hated opponents disintegrate with lovely regularity. Our stars remain undimmed and uninjured. Classic goals stand unmolested by pedantic offside decisions. Our free kicks rocket home; their penalties are superbly saved. Instead of struggling to succeed against the odds, we are odds-on for the Double. Amidst all this, we cling to Eric for the saviour that he is; the greatest nomad since Moses responds by nailing his future to the United banner. Could life be any more perfect?

Well, maybe .... I have heard the first whispers of "Lucky United" growled in Scouse and Tyke accents in the way we used to moan "Lucky Arsenal". It's not a label to be welcomed. Perversely I begin to yearn for that feeling of being up against it, of being persecuted, of extracting improbable triumphs from the jaws of seemingly inevitable defeat. A bit of bad luck wouldn't go amiss – as long as we still win in the end of course. As Hornby remarks, one of the best feelings in football is to go a goal down – preferably from a blatant offside position – when the team are playing well; the sense of injustice and anticipation of an avenging fight-back is fire to the soul. So of course I still want us to clinch the Double at Wembley in May but I'd rather luck played no part. Let us concede two dodgy penalties and be down to ten men before we win 3-2 in injury time after fighting savagely for every yard. Now that's what I call United.

(Dec. 93)

How to worry a flock of virgin sheep: show them this picture

Part Five:

FOREIGN LESIONS

1. Turkey-Shoot
2. Dante's Inferno
3. Gothenberg '94
4. Always Look On The Bright Side ...
5. USA '94 – UK '95?
6. When Irish Eyes Aren't Smiling
7. The Italian Job

TURKEY-SHOOT

Galatasaray away in 93/94 was an unmitigated disaster all-round and not an event that did much to correct the world's 'Midnight Express' view of the Turks. The serious coverage in the fanzines was excellent and a reminder of their importance at key moments; within a couple of months, in typically Mancunian style, we felt more able to take a more black-humoured view of the Ottoman onanists.

Yes, yes, I know it was some time ago and we've all been studiously trying to forget what happened but every time I see a Champions League table with that dreaded name "Galatasaray" in it, I still feel intensely aggrieved. Admittedly, on the basis of what actually happened on the pitch, they deserved to be there but one only has to watch the pre-second leg footage from the United video to see that the total lack of Western civilisation in Turkey created such an angst in the United team that what followed was scarcely sport as we know it. What they did to our fans alone merited their exclusion from the cup as a nation unfit to receive visitors.

In any case, what are Turkish teams doing in the European Cup anyway? Technically a small percentage of the country is geographically in our continent but basically Turkey is a huge Middle Eastern slavering beast that has one of its buttocks accidentally draped over the intercontinental fence. Politically and spiritually, they're nothing to do with Europe. It seems to me that they're trying to wheedle their way into Europe and the EC so they can spend the next century living off Euro subsidies whilst continuing to behave like some tinpot Third World dictatorship. United fans are not the only ones to get treated like infidel barbarians over there; look what happened to the UK trade unionists there recently and witness the persecution of the Kurdish minority over the years. Listen, over here we tend to believe in the rule of law, human rights and not treating sport as an extension of warfare, so if you can't behave yourselves, get the f*ck out of our sight!

History should have told us to expect this sort of thing. Who did the Turks pick to play alongside in the Championships of 1914-18 and 1939-45? The Germans. To err once like that is forgivable; twice demonstrates that you are an arse. What happened when our own Lawrence of Arabia went over there to play for Arabs United against the Turkish Ottomans in 1917? They reacted to a thumping defeat by putting him in a cell and rogering him senseless all night long. Not very sporting. Eric may have been unhappy about being hit by a police truncheon but at least he didn't find a Turkish pink torpedo up his bottom. More recently, a dispute in 1974 on Cyprus about whether Galatasaray or AEK Athens were the better team ended nastily when the Turkish Army in true Bitter fashion invaded the pitch and have been there ever since.

No, it can't be allowed to continue. Individual Turks are great – those blokes in the city centre who run kebab houses draped with United flags are a case in point – but as a nation they're a menace to European standards of fair play. United know better than most what it's like to play in a hostile atmosphere and our fans have had their fair share of police harassment but we have got to draw the line at being expected to perform in a war zone. Unless they apologize and give our lads full compensation, the club should give notice now that we will refuse to play in Istanbul again and challenge UEFA to get it sorted .

That Turkish Delight always did make me spew ...

(Jan. 94)

DANTE'S INFERNO

Somewhere in the Bible, it says procrastination is a sin – what it doesn't explain is that such fannying about is punishable by condemnation to an Official Manchester United plc away trip, which is what Dante had in mind when he talked of the 'outer circles of hell.' I'd delayed my Barcelona application to UF tours for so long that I'd missed the boat (as well as the plane and coach) and was thus forced to hand over £229 to the Club for a day trip and a guaranteed Nou Camp ticket. Too much of a pussy to risk making my own way there and find a richly-ticketed tout, that seat guarantee was the only consolation during a day that utterly disproves the old adage 'It's better to travel than arrive.' By 10.30, of course, I was wishing that I hadn't f*cking arrived at all – but let's not go into that 90 minutes of purgatory again please ....

Apparently, the club ended up running a total of twelve planes to Barcelona, of which seven left on the day of the game itself from Manchester. By ten a.m., terminal 1 at Manchester airport was filled with seven sprawling queues of Reds, as if seeking entry through check-in desk turnstiles to an invisible stadium. A brief sociological scan of the Red-shirted hordes revealed the official party to be a strangely skewed cross-section of an Old Trafford crowd – the young girls, grannies, Club Class smarties and family groups were all there in abundance but "the lads" were somehow understrength. Resignedly realising that UF tours had probably creamed off the 'Red Issue'-type elite, I prepared myself for a day of tedium. In the departure lounge, a few desperate cries of 'K-Stand's Barmy Army' went up, met with even fewer desultory replies of 'J-stand', which served only to confirm that most of you, dear readers, were elsewhere.

At midday, a frisson of distaste rippled through the lounge when Martin Edwards pranced through. As he headed for his scheduled flight, an irate K-Stander shouted over 'So it's all right for you to travel unofficial is it?' Fartin' had the grace to blush before scuttling off as the air filled with bitter denunciations of the entire Barcelona trip scenario. I hesitate to call the trip a 'rip-off' as the Evening News have received a libel writ from United for doing just that but when you compare the prices with either UF tours or the going rate for Barcelona mini-breaks, you can only conclude that someone, somewhere was making a pile out of us. In today's paper, I see an ad: two nights in decent accommodation in central Barcelona including flights for £154. The official day-trip cost more than that just for the flight. Johnny Flacks from the FSA was there, still fuming about the treatment meted out on Sunday to United supporters by

Brittany Ferries. He was compiling a dossier on the entire subject of clubs and monopoly travel schemes and had calculated that someone was making close to £70 a head profit on the day-trip alone. The club, naturally, had licensed the whole deal to a third party so that no-one can know who exactly is making what; they are allowed to get away with this enforced monopoly by hiding behind the UEFA rules which were never meant to sanctify such rampant profiteering. One soft lad suggested the extra cost was justified by the fact that 'security' had been provided but we worked out, after slyly questioning the suits themselves, that the extra cost amounted to £3 a head. What a racket – Al Capone would have been impressed.

Ah, the suits. Half-a-dozen to a plane, seemingly selected from an assortment of dodgy night-club doorways and various primary schoolyards, such was the disparity in age and appearance. As they strutted around the terminal, they exuded authority and responsibility in their natty casual sports-wear – 'Aha!'. By the end of the day, it was clear that the only things that distinguished them from us were a) their blazers and b) their ability to get themselves some duty free on the plane back. Their only 'authority' was over us; the varieties of Spanish officialdom treated them with utter disdain. They had less clout than your average package holiday tour rep; had they not been there, it wouldn't have made the slightest difference to the day's events.

The planes carrying the Red invasion force did at least take off on time – a fleet of Monarch 757s whose vibrational tendencies caused some nervous banter at V1-speed: "I'd pay good money to get this sensation in Blackpool ... or at a massage parlour" etc etc. The stars of the day were the airline staff who, as it turned out, performed far better than the team. Top nosebag, smart service, decent laughs on the video screens and hostesses who showed admirable forbearance in dealing with excitable Reds who had been denied the usual relaxant qualities of alcohol. Might I just indulge myself here to abuse the prat in 34f on plane 6; your 90-decibel running commentary throughout both flights was so entirely witless, embarrassing and irritating that it constituted the perfect argument for enforced sterilisation

Emerging blinking, sober and perspiring into the arrivals hall at Barcelona airport, an expectant bevy of film-crews were there to meet us, no doubt hoping for some telegenic examples of British lager lout behaviour. Unfortunately we didn't even raise a song: this was like being on tour with the G-stand grandads. The 'organizers' had already made their first mistake in allowing everyone to dash for the massed ranks of coaches and get on any they fancied, an oversight which caused mammoth delays later that night. We'd already been given match tickets on the plane but had also been told that anyone not getting on the coach would not be guaranteed admission. This was enough to put off all but the bravest and was, of course, a complete crock of shit. It was an opportunity to 'escape' that was to be much regretted by all we obedient sheep.

Half an hour later, we were at the Nou Camp, having first crossed the Placa de Catalunya where Barca fans were beginning to congregate, happy to be in time to give us the finger and shout scoreline predictions at us. 'Three-nil' yelled one sadly-dressed shrimp on a moped. Oh, how we laughed at his rabid optimism ...

The stadium looked eminently unimpressive as we drove past before being corralled into a 'coachpark' that was even worse than OT's. We didn't realise that the concentric circles of the stadium tiers plunge deep below ground level until you reach a truly subterranean pitch – as Dante again would have it, a pit of hell in which even the Red Devils would find only torture and death. Chaos ensued in the coach park – a 20 minute delay capped by the suits telling us to get back on board, only to be immediately countermanded by puzzled police who told us we could proceed. It rapidly became obvious that the suits were flusteredly floundering out of their depth – not one of them spoke a word of Spanish and several had apparently never been into Europe before. Good choice, United.

We expected to have to run a gauntlet of Barca hoolies but instead found a smattering of kids hugely outnumbered by ranks of Spanish pigs, resplendent in penis-substitute mega-truncheons and tight trousers. We were already at the away fans' entrance and kick-off was still more than three hours away. Time to explore, have a drink and a song, right? Wrong. The police set up an amateurish cordon and insisted we all enter the stadium pronto. The suits, having received their 'orders', promptly tried to shove us in. Furious rows broke out as Reds demanded to be free to enjoy the build-up just like all the other Reds who'd been in Barcelona for ages – we'd passed a large coterie of Reds outside a bar just minutes away on the coach. A lad called Vinny became the instant fans' spokesman, haranguing the hapless suits for several minutes as I stood by with tape recorder in hand. From my broken Spanish conversation with the pig-chief it was obvious that the suits only had to unite and demand we be released and he'd have given in. No such luck. Within ten minutes, three thousand Reds were climbing the ramps into our top tier section with kick-off hours away and the stadium empty.

You have to admit that your first sight of the Nou Camp as you emerge through the boca into the top tier is breathtaking. TV pix and photos don't do it justice – it is truly awe-inspiring. Old Trafford is in comparison a nicely-shaped foothill next to the Himalayan mountain that is the Nou Camp. The view partially compensated for having to spend so much time cooped up in their crappy concourse served by 'facilities' that would disgrace the Endsleigh sheds. Outside the ground, way way below, we could spy the suits pacing shabbily around the car park. Stories circulated about the rank wankiness of the official trips; those who'd arrived on Tuesday told of cancelled trips and tours, handicapped fans having to fend for themselves and even a suit who couldn't find his own hotel. Lads who'd been with UF tours before and had expected 'superior' packaging from the official trips said they'd never make the mistake again. Still, at least we were there and in; I wondered how the 'independents' were faring in their quest to gain entry – at least they'd have had a good time getting here.

Kick-off approached – we looked good spread across the top tier in a manner that brought back reminiscences of Rotterdam. Replays of the 2-2 shimmered on the giant screen as Barca fans slowly filled out the enormous bowl. The cage to our right, presumably UF tours, created a volume of noise out of all proportion to its size but the performance of the official 3,000 was patchy at best, provoking some in the cage to bellow 'make some f*cking noise you twats'. By the 60th minute, no-one was

HOW WAS IT FOR YOU?.....

shouting anything beyond the odd encouragement to Giggs to head for the San Siro. What can you say? I don't want to talk about it. It was like being forced to watch your girlfriend being gang raped by Leeds fans. Stunned and horrified, we just wanted to get back to the plane, go home and mourn.

Held behind for aeons and treated to a final insult as two locals unveiled a 'Barca-Leeds' scarf, we were finally released from purgatory and bombed back to the airport. Once there, with the first take-off imminent, the stupidity of allowing a coach free-for-all became apparent as the planes were forced to wait for every coach to arrive before they could get a take-off slot. Further inexplicable delays occurred in coach parking and off-loading which seemed only to add to the mad scrummaging in the airport. Many were in my position – on a coach held back till last for no reason but supposed to be on the first flight out for which the last call was being announced as we approached security control. Unbelievably, the sadistic Spanish insisted on doing a full metal check, creating a massive hold-up. Protests to the suits were useless – they had clearly been given no authority to smooth our passage at any point. Some indeed simply used their position to bundle to the front of the queue so that at least they would be OK should the planes decide to depart. Once on board, they also made sure they got their duty-free despite the fact that the rest of us were denied it due to 'lack of time'. We drowned our sorrows in Beck's and complimentary wine, cursed Edwards and marvelled at the brilliance of Stoichkov and Romario. Home at 2:30, depressed and defeated – and never to be a day-tripper again for sure. I'll walk to Goteborg if necessary.

(Nov. 94)

MATCH REPORT: GOTHENBERG AWAY, 23rd NOVEMBER 1994

A godforsaken railway station on the Danish coast somewhere around 6 a.m., the ridiculously early morning after the night before. The tightly-knit pack of Reds stuffed into the solitary, unlit train carriage haven't actually been in a bed for 24 hours and it's that time when the prodigious, record-breaking volumes of alcohol consumed before and after the match are beginning to induce near-comatose states in the occupants. You know that stage: you can sleep in virtually any location, in any position, as long as some well-meaning fellow-traveller Swede isn't babbling commiserations and his life story down your lughole. When the hapless buffoon tries to look on the bright side by pointing out the mathematical possibilities of United's qualification, the two semi-slumbering fanzine editors who are listening to their mate and the Swede's discussion make their definitive statements on whether United deserve to proceed. "No. We're shite" says one, before collapsing back onto the headrest. "We're fucking shite," fine-tunes the other as he disappeared under his fantastically silly IFK ski-hat. As Nutty Norm would say, it was as simple as that. To lose appallingly badly in Europe once can be forgiven – but twice? Twice looks not just like carelessness, as Oscar Wilde might contend, but rank crappiness of an unforgivable order. Deprived of the stimulant buzz of a victory, returning Reds all over northern Europe sank into the depressed drunken stupor of defeat. Wake us up when we're European Champions will you?

"You know what really gets me?" asked Lance rhetorically as we headed back down Ullevistadt, "I honestly never thought we could lose. Barcelona away, OK, you're half-prepared for it. But here? Here?! This is even worse than the four-nil. I'm just ... just ... gutted." He'd found the mot juste alright.

Is there anything in the cosmos that can so devastatingly alter the mood of so many in such a short time as a bad football result? Two hours previously, thousands of multi-national Reds were reaching the apex of drunken, adrenalined pre-match euphoria to which we had been climbing relentlessly since the first arrivals in Scandinavia on Sunday and Monday. Once again, it had indeed turned out to be better to travel than arrive.

After the Champions League fixture list was announced back in the summer, this particular tie had behaved in advance like its Swedish hosts – shy, self-effacing and huddling almost ignored in the huge shadow cast by the prospects of the much-hyped visits to Barca and Istanbul. Now, thanks to the Catalonian catastrophe and the unexpectedly good showing of IFK themselves, the Ullevi match had been transformed into a quasi-Cup tie, a throwback to the good, bad and ugly days of sudden death on foreign fields. Essentially, we needed a win, though a draw could still suffice depending on other teams' results, the conjunction of the Moon and Uranus etc. etc. However, one thing was utterly certain and should have been branded on every player's forehead lest his colleagues forget: DO NOT LOSE. Defeat would leave us facing odds against qualification of National Lottery proportions or even instant elimination. But hey, we're the greatest team the world has ever seen, right? A team of hardened, disciplined, sumptuously-paid professionals with Euro-fire in their bellies, n'est-ce pas? Surely defeat against an assortment of herring-chomping journeymen whom we had so recently put four goals past would be incredible even within the confines of a 'Brookside' script? Understand, then, that the thousands of Red Army invaders lurching across the North Sea were buzzing as much on the stimulant of confident anticipation as off the effects of the duty-free. A mini-European Cup Final watched by a proper gathering from Planet United against a team of soft, late-goal-slimers: a mouth-watering menu in Montpellierian style. Ha.

Not that everyone was going to be at the feast, of course. In the run-up to the game, the same sad lament sprang from many Red lips around town: "Can't go, mate – all spent up in Barca" or occasionally with cruel irony "I'm starting to save for Paris St. Germain in March." Too many Red wallets were afflicted with fiscal-sexual dysfunction – they'd shot their loads too quickly and it was too soon to get it up again. Pleasingly, this did at least mean that the MUFC Official Tour was having trouble selling seats and was still pleading for customers at the Palace game, which was hardly surprising given the experiences of many on their trip to Barca. For those determined this time to plough their own furrow, the usual obstacles remained, although tickets were at least slightly easier to come by in advance than those for the Nou Camp had been. Scandinavian Ferries meanwhile were aping their gutless colleagues at Brittany by refusing to take any footie fans anywhere that week; people who'd booked weeks in advance were getting calls from the company cancelling their reservations on the slightest pretext, with 'being from Manchester' apparently condemnation enough.

UF Tours took a full complement on their one-night package, still able to find ample customers despite the reported failings on their Barca trip; others, such as the vanguard from the Red Issue/United We Stand elite, took as fiercely independent a line as possible by sorting tickets from IFK and travelling as leisurely and luxuriously as possible via Copenhagen and its fleshpots.

That, of course, is only half the story. Just as in the mass population removal that was the Red expedition to Spain, Gothenberg was the Naked City, full of a thousand stories. Haggard individual reds, clumped together in little raiding parties, told the usual myriad tales of the bonkers itineraries, illegal manoeuvres and shameless free-loading that constituted their own voyages. United habitually by shared ticketlessness and poverty, somehow the dedicated lumpenproletariat had made it, as they always do. Some Brummie Reds had managed to stowaway on a container ship before blagging tickets by pretending to be the Midlands Branch of the IFK Blue Angels; one Londoner with whom the police are keen to speak in four different countries had sneaked through with the aid of three false passports; a group of particularly wasted Mancs had taken five days to get there, having broken down, crashed or had vans robbed during a journey-total of fifteen unforeseen stoppages. Most impressive of all was the Salford lad who claimed to have scored with five different women en route, each of whom then drove him another stage towards Sweden so that he'd got there for free. Those disinclined to believe him were later horrified to see him leave the Bryggeriet with two Andersonian blonde babes ...

After travelling to Barca with the 'officials' and vowing never to repeat the experience, I took the diametrically opposed route of hitching up with the 'fanzine' tour who were wending their way through Denmark to get to Gothenberg for Tuesday afternoon. Somewhere en route, I picked up a copy of 'The Sun' which had a story about the beer consumption of the touring Australian rugby team who had apparently demolished 16,000 tinnies during their stay in Britain. This was supposed to be a gastronomic feat of Guinness Book magnitude but a few hours of observation and some quick calculations led me to conclude that the Aussies are virtual teetotallers in comparison to the legendary behemoths who were imbibing entire bars all around. The greatest shock to the system for all those arriving in Scandinavia had, of course, been the price af beer. It's all very well having megastrength Elephant beer on draft wherever you go but when it's six or seven quid a pint, you begin to hanker for your local Boddies emporium. Not that this dissuaded Mick, Chris, Phil and their cohorts from establishing 12-hour sessions across the centres of Copenhagen and Goteborg during which the amount of wedge passing over the bar must have exceeded the GDP of small African nations. Somebody had indeed remarked beforehand that it would be as well to 'have your drinking legs on' but he'd neglected to mention the large reservoir-cum-septic tank that needed to be affixed to the stomach as well. Monday night in Copenhagen, for those who could remember it amongst the fanzine crew, swag-peddlars and assorted stragglers who were around, was a titanic effort: everybody got completely sunk. With the prescience of the knowledgeable traveller, several revellers also made the most of the red light delights, aware that Gothenberg held little in the way of actual sensual pleasures – not, at least, of those for which you pay. One or two of the luckier lads got close enough to the Danish sex-goddesses who abounded in disconcerting numbers to fall instantly in love; the consensus seemed to be that the Swedish Agnethas would be a much tougher proposition for the budding Casanovas amongst us, so now was the moment to dispense the Ribbed Featherlites.

Let's face it: Gothenberg is not the first city Dionysus would've picked for a weekend of debauched excess. Travelling to the centre from the airport, the place appeared to be something like St. Petersburg with money; bleak, uniform, almost grandiose but hardly welcoming. Appallingly, the beer was even more expensive than in Denmark and the women that bit less impressed by leery Mancunian beer-monsters than the Danes. The carnally-obsessed found to their disappointment that the second city of the ultimate porn-exporting nation had a red light district that consisted of two sex shops and one slightly disreputable bar. Everywhere else was clean, polite, proper and passion-less, with a local populace to match; even the most low-rent bars wouldn't have been out of place in the glossiest environs of Manchester's city centre. Inveterate sight-seers who had at least found the Little Mermaid and the hippy commune in Copenhagen soon realised that Gothenberg's fish-gutting factories hardly constituted essential visits and joined the rest of the assembling Red clans in the downtown bars, busy spending their life savings. Six quid a pint in a bar, not that much cheaper in the System-bollaget off-licenses which are only open till 6pm, age restrictions everywhere that can bar even 23 year-olds ... what is it with Swedes and booze that makes them vote for governments which try to stop them doing what they clearly enjoy as much as the next man? A local smugness claimed "we use the booze taxes to support our great welfare state, so we pay up happily in bars" but this is clearly bollocks. Sweden used to be a nation of complete alcoholics, like modern Russia but with more suicides, when beer was cheap in the 1930s – the taxes are surely there to prevent them from a) drinking themselves into comas b) littering the roads with smashed-up Volvos and c) getting brewer's droop in the midst of a porn-flick-shoot. All very typically Swedish and sensible but how about cut-price drinks for us impoverished tourists? We don't mind the odd lager-coma ...

Nevertheless, there are twenty-two decent bars inside one square kilometre in central Goteborg and by Tuesday evening, Reds could be found in most of them. (I know, because in the interests of research, I toured them all.) The first plane and train loads had arrived mid-afternoon with another consignment to follow at around ten p.m.; the preponderance of Sharp tops marked out the new arrivals from the colour-free hard-core who'd got there early. The first arrests soon followed, police touring the city to pick up a collection of alleged forgers who'd been trying to off-load dodgy twenties. If these were the same reprobates who'd been trying to do the same up and down the Warwick Road before the Palace game, good riddance; ripping off fanzine sellers and barrow lads is neither big nor clever. Still, you can't help but reflect that ten years ago, the scene would have been much different, doubtless dominated by bunches of fives rather than rolls of twenties.

Of course, precisely those guys who would have been the ones wielding the fists ten years ago were all there in Gothenberg, despite the efforts of all those security agencies with their 'banned hoolies' lists. Long-serving Cockney Reds paced warily around many a plush hotel lobby, instantly identifiable by the London-smart threads, glinting of gold bracelets and the fact that the more subtly-attired Mancs were ignoring them. Plus ça change. Quietly intense Northern lads sitting in bar corners would be revealed by companions as 'X, from the Chelsea kick-off' or 'Y, back from a Valencian jail', lads whose troubled lives still had to find time for the Reds in Europe. Amidst the hordes of young lads for whom Dave Sexton is just a name from bedtime horror stories, these older characters whose faces speak of past lives in a very different football universe provided the moment with a sense of historic, if uneasy, continuity.

Sometime during Tuesday night, the 'Auld Dubliner' Irish-style pub off the Kungsportsplats was designated the unofficial HQ of the invading Reds by virtue of the usual subconscious and/or telepathic process that occurs at aways. With the triple-tiered 'Gamle Port' and 'O'Leary's' ' only yards away, hundreds of Reds were to venture no further than this little corner of a foreign field, forever British. Well, rather more than British actually: as the place began to pack out once more during Wednesday lunch-time, it became clear that the clarion call for Red support had been heeded well beyond our own island borders. Masses of Norwegians and Danes plus a smattering of Germans, Stockholmian Swedes and other assorted foreigners had also made the pilgrimage; it was rumoured that a pub in the north of the city had 500 mad Oslo Reds in it, doing exactly what their emissaries in the 'Dubliner' were: singing our songs in bizarre accents, throwing in their own hurdy-gurdy anthems, getting as pissed as possible and taking their once-in-a-lifetime chance to schmooze with real Manc Reds.

Their motivation was admirable; said a Dane to me, "I'm here because I love United like I love my mother and because I f*cking hate the

Swedes." However accustomed you think you are to the phenomenon of the Red Planet, it is still a shock to hear a 20 year-old from Dusseldorf discuss the relative demerits of Paddy Roche and Tommy Jackson in English apparently learned from British football commentaries. There is perhaps something slightly disconcerting about these adherents of United internationalism. Sometimes you feel that foreigners supporting the Reds so fervently is a bit, well, 'cousin-kissing' if you see what I mean: technically legitimate but morally uncertain in a vaguely nauseous way. Perhaps all that City Manc-centrism crap has had its effect and spoiled what should be the unalloyed joy of nations uniting under a Red Flag. Whatever, the lads being offered a hundred krone for their United Members badges by drunken Swedish Reds weren't complaining – although the burly Stockport Red who found himself being repeatedly smothered in slobby kisses by a German Red shouting "I love you Manchester" had probably had enough entente cordiale for one day.

Wednesday afternoon in the 'Dubliner.' Kick-off is five hours away but both levels are crammed. Downstairs, an impromptu vocal concert is underway, conducted in Pete Boyle's enforced absence by the Cantona lookalike who's now called 'Eric' by all and enjoined by masses of beered-up celebrants. It seems like the whole of K-stand has squeezed itself in although most under-20s have been barred and forced to trot down the Avenyn to find bars to drain dry. Two hours pass by in the flash of an alcoholic daydream but the singers refuse to let up; tables are overturning, the floor is carpeted in glass and the bar is "doing a week's business in an hour" to quote the delightful pump-maiden. Sporadically, knots of police force their way in to gaze upon the Bacchanalian scene, barely able to suppress the huge grins that such gatherings always induce in observers. "So, where are the English hooligans then?" asks one. "Back in Leeds, mate," comes the instant reply. The pig laughs out loud – it was that kind of day. Outside, clutches of bemused Swedes look in through the windows and stand gawping for aeons as the Edgeley Reds put on a show for them; "Welcome to the EEC" yells one topical wit. And welcome to nineties away trips: the crack is everything, the beer, strumpets and song – "among the thugs" is no more.

With a slightly tactless chorus of "No Surrender to the IRA" and a "Rule Britannia" finale, the 'Dubliner' disgorged its drunken but buzzing masses who headed unsteadily for the Ullevi Stadium a mere ten minutes stagger away. IFK fans materialized as if from nowhere to join the match-bound throng, bantering politely in soft-edged Scandinavian style with the Red-bedecked Danes and Norwegians who were tagging along with us. The Ullevi is only used for the bigger games, IFK being unable to fill it for clashes with the likes of Smorgasbord Athletic; tonight, their own versions of the day-trippers and part-timers had turned up, drawn as much by the lustre of United as by the prospects of qualification. Face-painted twelve-year olds are, it seems, a universal currency these days.

The Ullevi works like the Nou Camp in reverse; stunningly impressive in a Star Trek kind of way from the outside with its modernistic architecture and roller-coaster roof but mundanely terrestrial within. Cursed by that bane of Euro-stadia, the pitch-side athletics track, parts of it look like Endsleigh league transplants with exits and 'gangways' from a pre-Taylor world of death. Most worryingly, the pitch looked to be about as playable as Fred West's garden, as bad even as Old Trafford's in the winter of 91/92 – not a good omen at all. And for the first time during our stay, the weather was beginning to live up to its billing i.e. bollock-freezing for us but almost skinny-dipping weather for our hardy hosts. (Shivering up on the top terrace, completely surrounded by IFK, I thought fondly of the body-stocking a lad had displayed under his kit in the pub; "borrowed it off me bird" he had beamed, although his mate later told me the bloke wore it for kicks whatever the temperature ...) Sad soothsaying types like me take climate changes seriously. Remember how weeks of windy weather came to an abrupt end on the day Hughes scored his Wembley volley and how it didn't really piss down again until the Final – just as it was raining goals on the pitch? Alright, maybe you don't, but the sudden onset of a soul-biting chill minutes after kick-off in the Ullevi spoke symbolic volumes to me.

At least United fans could sense they were part of the stadium this time, unlike in Barca where the dizzy heights of our encampments made you feel you were celestial observers of the crowd, not participants in it. The 'officials' had turned up in sufficient numbers to constitute an impressive-looking presence to the right of the goal where Hughesy scored; at the other end, three distinct legions had formed. The UF Tours crowd took the right flank, the massed Scandinavian Reds had seized the left, whilst the core crew from the fanzine tour had planted themselves directly behind the goal, shoving the Swedes in their section behind them. The emblem of 'unofficial' United abroad, the 'United We Stand' flag, was proudly affixed to the fence and with the eventual arrival of a certain fanzine editor, fresh from three days luxury in the Sheraton, all the familiar elements were in place. Unfortunately, so was David May.

Of course, it would be invidious and cruel to blame one individual for so clearly a team effort as the subsequent disaster but with Davey boy, you just can't help yourself. Within a minute, he'd committed his first blundering foul of the night, causing the free-kick which led to Hughesy's booking and consequent suspension: within ten minutes, it was obvious to all that Blomqvist would have enough energy left after repeatedly savaging May to give Brucey a few duffings-up too. All season, May's tender flesh at right back had been exposed by domestic strikers – but only bit-by-bit, as if no-one had the heart to rip off his ill-fitting clothes in one denuding swoop. Young Jesper had no such qualms; when you find the right back slot filled by a mere ginger-tinged hole in the air, you make the most of it. By half-time – well, by the twenty minute mark actually – Reds in our end were howling for May to get off the pitch by any means possible. When it looked as though he was getting a yellow card, one traumatized Red yelled "make it red! make it red!". That's some recommendation of awfulness when a fan reckons a team is better off a man down than with you still on board.

By this point, we were already a goal down. It was symptomatic of the night's cruelty that May had, for once, stepped up with the rest of the line and yet, unbelievably, 'dependable Denis' had played the scorer on. Perhaps he'd expected May to make the tackle? – bad call, Bogman, you should've sussed the score with delicate Dave by now ... and more portents of doom followed. McClair and Andrei both had the sort of chances you'd seen them put away a dozen times a season, but not tonight. Choccy's little looped header found Ravelli's fingers instead of dribbling across the goal-line as is usual; Andrei chose to flick at his effort instead of drilling it unstoppably home as he'd been doing all autumn. Elsewhere, unaccustomed sights abounded – Incey unable to stamp his authority on midfield, Eric trying desperately to wield an influence and dropping ever deeper in his forlorn quest, Hughes being bundled off the ball with depressing regularity et cetera, et bloody cetera. IFK may not be a brilliant side but at least they were showing form, playing like a unit and keeping their cool. By contrast, we looked as ragged, ill and hot-tempered as a Souness side and Eric in particular seemed as if he was heading for an Istanbulian tantrum. Half-time came as a relief, as some half-expected a Nou Camp-style second just before the break – at least at only 0-1 we had the chance to effect running repairs and save us from yet another continental calamity.

Stunned perhaps by the appalling vista of elimination that was opening up before us, our support had not been at vintage levels with the UFT contingent being especially disappointing after their sterling efforts in Barca. The locals were not much better with only their version of K-stand, the 'Blue Angels' to our top left, displaying much vocal talent. Their indecipherable, pause-strewn chants were impressively coherent on the occasions that they did get it together but were met with blank responses from the rest; the OT syndrome of day-tripper-dilution seemed to be at work. We spent half-time plotting May's assassination, laughing at the intoxicated locals falling over and, in big R.'s case, thumping annoying Swedes who insisted on shoving flags in our faces. A collection of Swedish babes fronted a marching band, who stopped in front of the main stand to display their pert little bottoms in a dance for the assembled season-ticket holders; our kind of executive privilege indeed and rather better entertainment than the arse-show we get at OT in Fred the Red. However, the main half-time consolation was that the second half couldn't be worse – and for precisely nineteen minutes, it wasn't. Slowly, deliberately but distinctly, we climbed our way back from the precipice edge in every way. Some semblance of passing began to occur on the pitch and half chances began to materialize; on the terraces, the officials started redeeming themselves for their Nou Camp no-show, inspiring our end to rouse ourselves once more. The stately, drawled "Yooo-nyyy-tid" that comes so naturally when you're alcoholically challenged was replaced by the urgent, repeated, staccato "United", a sure sign that life is speeding up to a climax which duly and deservedly arrived in the 64th minute with a goal of pure simplicity. May to Eric's head, down to Hughes and in the net for 1-l ... how ridiculously easy it looked after an hour of ham-fisted labouring. Predictably, ecstatic scenes ensued, as you would expect when your entire universe has been transformed in a split-second. Hughes had done for our Euro-season what he had for our double last April; our beloved, heroic leader had saved us all once more. Hadn't he?

Such was the cruelty of that night that even a momentary celebration wasn't allowed to last out the moment itself. I for one barely had time to clear my vision, lift my head out of my neighbour's frenzied embrace and look up to watch the bedlam at the officials' end when I caught sight of May careering towards us in hopeless pursuit of a Swedish winger; the instant he was disgracefully allowed to cross the ball, everything began to go black around the edges of my vision, like the close of some 1930s movie. The ball was in the net, 'The End' was on the screen and our European dream had become a nightmare from which you can't awaken.

The rest was supremely irrelevant. At the moment when United's performance had sobered up and begun to walk, we had been smashed all over the road by a juggernaut. May, at last, was hauled off to spare him and us further humiliation down the flank but in a typically ironic moment, it was his replacement Neville whose slip led to the penalty which made it three-one seven minutes later. Nineteen minutes of hope at the start of the half gave way to a final nineteen minutes of hell. We had chances but none were ever going to go in from the moment they were struck, not on a night like this. Nor did we deserve otherwise; Ince's sending off for his introduction to the Italian ref of East End vernacular vocab added an extra, final brushstroke of shame to the gruesome picture, as if any more were needed. Most of us weren't even aware he'd gone until hours later which tells you something about a) the catatonic state we were in and b) the lack of impact Ince was having on the game anyway.

As is apt for such a huge, dramatic club, when we f*ck up we really f*ck it up big-style don't we?

A minute to go. Defeat is now mathematically certain and, as far as we knew for several hours yet, so is elimination. The Swedes are doing – gulp – a Mexican wave, that ultimate symbol that you've been outclassed and are having the piss taken although the locals don't do it with malicious intent. The Swedes have behaved impeccably towards us throughout and there are words of consolation for us that are actually sincere. The players later declare that they want to beat Barca to help United and you believe them. A few local wannabees try to taunt us from the safety of their moving cars but being verbally attacked by a Swede is like being savaged by a dead herring, as Dennis Healey might say. There's no outlet for your disgusted disillusion or your bitter anger here but the bartap. There is no trouble, no street clamour, no hostility; the scores of circling panda cars are to be obsolete. I pass by the 'Dubliner' to which the beaten have retreated; the songs are still being sung and the glasses drained but the atmosphere has changed from stag night to funeral reception. The 'f*ck-it-let's-party' black humoured joie de vivre of Barcelona's aftermath is much harder to summon up now; "we only lost three-one" doesn't quite have the same ring does it? Those of us who are heading back that night are grateful for the speedy exit – there's no wish to linger at the scene of death, however much we might dread the gleeful reaction of the Bitters & Co. back home. Draining the dregs of the duty-free on the night ferry, we know that notwithstanding the lifeline offered by the Barca result, we are out; no spring trips to Paris, no San Siro show-downs, no Rotterdamesque Final carnivals. As a consequence, we might all be financially better off come May but spiritually, we'll all be unspeakably poorer. Shit.

We meet a Swede on the way back who tells us he is 'quite pleased' by the result. To our suggestion that he's being rather understated about such a momentous victory, he replies that Swedes are a level-headed lot: "We don't really care that much about winning or losing, we just like to play the game." Spitting with frustrated incomprehension, Steve B. speaks for us all. "That's the trouble with you lot; you just don't know how it feels to be gutted. We are totally gutted. See?" That word again – it says it all.

Another lad related a story from his after-match drinking session. He'd actually come across a few Swedes who were up for a bit of wound-salting and he'd had enough of it. He decided to demonstrate to them what it means to be a United fan, what depth of feeling runs through Red veins. Briefly, he reminded them of the Munich disaster, then stood on a chair and sang the entire version of the unbearably poignant "Flowers of Manchester" with everything he had. "By the end, they were in total silence. Two of 'em were virtually in tears. That was the end of their piss-taking." And in that reminder of the stupidity of Shankly's famous maxim, I took the smallest of consolation. Football isn't more important than life or death; we'd lost a hugely important game but at least we were all going home relatively unscathed, including the drunk who'd fallen off the back of a Swedish train. Thirty-six years ago we'd had no such good fortune. We all use the words 'disaster' and 'catastrophe' to sum up our footballing lowlights but anyone with a feeling for this Club knows that all such terminology is relative. This team will, one day, be back in Europe to fight again – another never had the chance.

(From the author's "As The Reds Go Marching On ..."
first extracted in Red Issue)

ALWAYS LOOK ON THE BRIGHT SIDE ... OF ELIMINATION

By now you should have started to get over the World Cup qualifying Rotterdam Robbery; the sight of orange doesn't make you want to puke like it did and you can hear the word "German" without immediately thinking bastard referee". You still want to break Koeman's legs, but hey, that's OK.

Of course, as summer in the States approaches you'll feel the pang of regret like an amputated limb but at least it's not 1978 so we don't have to put up with any Tartan Army b*ll*cks. As the song says, the bright side demands your attention. Firstly, at least we'll be rid of Taylor. Imagine the humiliation we could have endured with the Turnip in charge in the US. Visualize 3-0 defeats by Nigeria, Carlton Palmer in every game and elaborate tactical plans featuring four centre backs and a Trapezium-shape midfield ... a lucky escape I think. At least we will be rid of him and his surreally ridiculous selections, instead of having him cling onto the job for years like an unwanted bogey.

"England fans" will be devastated, but should we care? Most of the hard-core support seem to be United-hating Southern scum with a nice line in Nazi politics and sad haircuts. Many support the national team because their clubs are so crap they'd never get away trips overseas if not through "supporting" England. All they ever seem to do is bugger things up for those of us who want to follow our clubs abroad, make a few mates and leave the locals with good memories of the Red Army. Instead we get greeted as if we were Viking raiders on a Rape 'n' Pillage away day. Cheers for all your ambassadorial work, England 'fans'. So your summer hols will need rearranging – try Benidorm.

Perversely, England's long term future may actually be better for our elimination. Taylor's successor will have three years without competitive matches to develop a new squad and style and won't have to cope with media hysterics and lynching parties every time we drop a point. In '96 we could well be in a position to win the Euro championships at home. Sheesh, several pigs just flew outta my butt ... Anyway, let's see this from the Red perspective which, after all, is the most important – surely United means more to us than England ever can? To be brutal, it's better for us that our England boys do not spend the last couple of months of the season dreaming about the US. You know, conserving their energy, making sure they don't get injured, playing to highlight themselves rather than for the team. Sounds terrible but it has been seen before. Now their pinnacle is going to be – hopefully – a Cup final or two and the title retention. England's loss, our gain.

(Dec. 93)

USA '94 - UK '95?

World Cups always set off fashionable little trends in footie around the globe, usually of the silliest sort; after Italia 90 and Roger Milla, no self-respecting forward could let a goal pass without carrying out some sort of porno-flick lambada by the corner flag, for example. So what about USA 94's legacy?

Poor Escobar, shot dead in Medellin after his own goal put Columbia out, gives us a promising precedent. Pampered footballers get bonuses for every conceivable reason – winning, scoring, league points, even attracting good attendances. But do they ever get done when they cock it up? Of course not. How about a sliding scale of physical punishments for crap displays? I could quite happily have put a couple of bullets through Waddle's shit haircut for his 1990 miss in Turin. Obviously execution should be reserved for particularly serious foul-ups but that still leaves plenty of scope for personally tailored punishment. Clayton Blackmore's nightmare in the New Years Day Massacre of '92 could have been dealt with by injecting him with a dose of the pox, forcing him out of bedroom action for a few weeks in the hope that his football might have improved. Neil Webb, lumbering around that season at his fattest, should clearly have been banged up in Strangeways for a fortnight and starved until his body began to resemble that of an athlete once more. Any more fumbling errors from Schmeichel should see him dispatched to spend a night naked in a Turkish baths with some randy lads from the Kurdish Liberation Front – that would certainly sharpen up his concentration in future.

Actually, Medellin sounds a familiar sort of place – full of drug cartels, gun-toting kids and filthy violent peasants. It's the South American Moss Side isn't it? If I were a City striker, I'd make sure I didn't miss any Derby day penalties next season or 'El Loco' Leroy might be waiting around the corner with redundant betting slips and an Uzi 9 millimetre ...

The other feature of USA that would amuse the Premiership would be the obscene celebration style of Nigeria. After one particular goal, the scorer ran over to the corner, got down on all fours and cocked a leg to feign urination. Honest, it was on BBC1. What a brilliant move! And he didn't get booked either. Apparently, as long as the celebrant doesn't gesture obscenely at the fans, such bawdy behaviour must be acceptable to FIFA. Perhaps we can expect Sharpe after scoring to peel away frantically simulating masturbation? Or Keano to stand aside a beaten goalie and pretend to drop a steaming turd on his face? Such antics would certainly liven up Match of the Day – "well, Alan, nice goal wasn't it? And a great doggy-sex impression from that big number nine ..."

What we don't want to see is anything like the puffery exhibited by Brazil, holding hands as they come out of the tunnel; with the slightest encouragement, Liverpool players might be all too keen to take the field in a daisy chain formation with their dicks shoved up each other's nether regions.

One trend we shouldn't expect the rest of the Premiership to pick up on is that of playing skilful, goalfest attacking football. That will, of course, continue to be the sole preserve of Man. United. Eat our shorts, suckers.

(Sept. 94)

WHEN IRISH EYES AREN'T SMILING ...

So yet another England awayday has ended in disgrace. If you were a non-football fan reading the media's Dublin coverage, you'd be forgiven for thinking this had come as a bolt from the blue, a virtually isolated reminder of the bad old days when no respectable family would be seen dead near a football stadium. The truth is, of course, that something like this has been on the cards for more than a year – all that was needed was a good opportunity, which the Irish FA helpfully provided by showering Dublin with blackmarket tickets. That the most visible outburst should occur at an England away game isn't a surprise; the last away game 17 months ago was studded with violence, so why should it have been any different the other week? The fact is that England away support has a greater proportion of psycho nutters than any individual club – to such a degree that it can never be assumed the 'responsible' majority will successfully suppress the extremists. An England gathering draws most of the headcases from most of the 'handiest' clubs; moreover, England acts as a particularly strong magnet for those to the right of Newt Gingrich. The result of those two processes is inevitable – an unusually numerous congregation of unusually right-wing white trash of unusually dominant influence. Given the special political circumstances in Dublin, an absence of rioting would have been miraculous. Only authorities as stereotypically dim as Ireland's could've been so complacent. (Incidentally, did anyone else find that Irish politician's gusto for slagging all Englanders as 'barbaric animals' rather aggravating? Coming from a nation that has harboured many covert supporters of murderous terrorists for 25 years, a touch less self-righteous generalization would've been in order ...)

What the media coverage demonstrated beyond all doubt was that those who are paid to be knowledgeable and to write about footie have no idea what's going on outside their cozy press-box world. Anyone who goes to away games in particular knows that aggro has been creeping steadily back over the last 18 months (and has, at last, begun to show up inside the stadia rather than confine itself to town centres or concourses.) And whereas once the media would jump on the slightest outbreak and hype it up, they have until recently engaged in a conspiracy of silence over the old voodoo's slight return. Why has recent aggro involving us at Elland Road, Anfield or Maine Road been so remarkably under-reported? Why are the media treating Dublin as the culmination of a very recent, short-term whirlwind that started at Selhurst Park (?!) and went via Ewood and Stamford before the exploding in Eire?

Personally, I suspect that the footie media have become too enthralled to the football establishment and the Brave New World of post-Taylorism. Writers and reporters have hitched themselves onto the family values/all seater/'good news' bandwagon and are happy to treat footie as an extension of Hollywood. They have realised what the new football audience of kids and mums wants to hear – lots of chirpy, happy, exciting stuff about glamour, superstars and pantomimesque heroes 'n' villains. And thanks to 'Fever Pitch' *et al*, you can be funny too – football is pure light ents, comedy for all, a laugh-a-game presided over by the modern-day Saint & Greavsie, Baddiel and Skinner. Above all, nothing must be written to spoil the image that the media, FA and Chairmen have struggled to create since the 80s – the world of football is a shiny, happy place for shiny, happy people.

So when incidents occur and trends emerge that threaten to undermine this vision, out come the editorial blue pens. Either that or the footie correspondents try to convince themselves that what they've just witnessed outside a pub, or the Nazi leaflets they've just seen distributed or the massed, 'foul-mouthed' crowd abuse they've just heard are simply isolated one-offs to be ignored and left unreported. For if they ever attempted to take a wider, long-term view of what's been developing, they'd realise that all is not as rosy as the image-makers' specs make football appear. And that's something they and the authorities don't wish to contemplate or see transmitted to the TV-watching public.

The result of such ostrich-like behaviour is that the truth becomes a casualty – and that important warnings go unheeded. For example, plenty of us have spent the best part of two seasons trying to agitate against the resurgent far-right threat and in particular that focused on the BNP and Combat 18. The national media, however, simply haven't wanted to know, with the honourable exception of Channel 4; now, after Dublin, the tabloids unite to treat Combat 18 as a national menace but one that has only just emerged. Talk about shutting doors after bolting horses – where were the tabloid Nazi-hunters when they were needed, right at the beginning, to nip the Nazis in the bud? Probably, in the Sun's case, too busy mouth-foaming against immigrants, bastard foreigners and their 'loony left' supporters. The Sun's directors are clearly either too thick or too cynical to reflect humbly on the irony here – the Sun and their ilk now engage in man-hunts to find tabloid-reading neo-Nazi thugs whose political education was largely gleaned from the very papers who now condemn them. Ha bloody ha.

Equally, the media aren't doing any favours for those 'innocent' families who are relatively new to football by applying such a Panglossian tinge to the footie experience. People attracted by the image of clean, family fun who are then traumatized by finding themselves in the midst of seething tribal passions must understandably feel they've been sold a false bill of goods. Any Red could have told a first-timer going into the so-called Family Stand at Selhurst that they were in for a high-decibel introduction to the full range of English obscenities but they'd have received no such warnings from the football industry and its image-makers. If Dublin and the other smaller-scale incidents have done any good, it will be to remind the public that football has not yet been fully surrendered to the thermos-toting families of tennis-club members.

Overall, the media have missed what could be the truly big story – that a backlash is in full swing against the post-Taylor settlement. This movement of opinion is not only against the new antiseptic world of all-seater stadia, family punters and commercialism – which most 'true' fans remain unenamoured with – but also seeks to revive a modus operandi that Heysel, Hillsborough and Taylor was supposed to have buried. There is now, more than ever, talk of old 'firms' reforming or of new ones being established; the word 'kick-off' is increasingly spoken in a context other than a 3pm start; there is renewed interest in the debris of cultural history relating to 'hooliganism' as evidenced by the success of 'Trouble on the Terraces'; and, of course, there is the undeniable re-emergence of the organized, footie-centred far right. Crucially, there is a sense of continuity too; there are, after all, plenty of individuals (and certain clubs – hello, Leeds) for whom violence never went out of fashion in the first place. If the older 'hoolie' is ready to take up cudgels once more, there are younger lads, for whom the 70s and 80s are ancient but glamourous history, who are equally ready to re-stage the blood-soaked scenes from the terrace stories their elders have brought them up on. Already those old media faves, the 'firm generals', are said to be back in action, organizing set-piece rucks for their troops and profiting from the distinct complacency shown by the authorities and media. At least Dublin will have changed one thing: footie aggro is now too good a news story for the footie media to allow themselves to ignore it 'for the good of the game', as they have done over the last couple of years.

It is now over ten years since the real 'hooligan decade' fizzled out, which is virtually a generation ago in football terms. The spirit of the times, the zeitgeist, is different to that which held sway in 86-90 when violence became rather 'uncool'. This is not the era of loved-up summers, dropping Es, the popped-up Roses, inflatables and the birth of the 'zines. The Roses have become heavy and sinister, crack has replaced E and a Mancunian summer is more likely to be sound-tracked by rattling Uzis than by blissed-out lovemaking. Different lads with different values make the running now; the 90s male's lifestyle and mindset, dominated by New Laddism rather than New Man-ism, are far more receptive to the Pulp Fiction brutalism that 'terrace' aggro requires. The transformation of the football experience into something akin to a theatre trip may yet be halted in its tracks.

(March 1995)

THE ITALIAN JOB

It's over-rated, over-hyped and over here – Italian football on Channel 4. But of course, most of us still watch it, even those invariably coma-inducing nil-nil draws on 'Mezzanotte'. After all, they're potentially United's opposition of the future, there's some top players on view and, well, it's footie innit? Better than the shite, typical-Sunday-afternoon film your missus wants to watch on BBC1 anyway (unless it is the actual 'Italian Job', naturally.) The question is, whom to support? Watching football as an appreciative neutral is the sort of sad thing your Dad does, so what features do United have in common with their various Clubs?

LAZIO

Pros: Italia 90 hero and, apparently, leading United fan Gazza played for them. Their support is phenomenal despite meagre success and, er, like United they're on the telly a lot.

Cons: They're the team of the Roman suburb 'country bumpkins', the Italian equivalent of the sheepshaggers. They were far too closely linked to Mussolini's fascists for the comfort of ideologically sound Reds – though there's more potential for a Leeds tie-in there. They play in exactly the same colours as the Bittermen and, spookily, haven't won a trophy for 19 years either. Verdict: Rejected.

NAPOLI

Pros: Even more fanatical support than Lazio. Like us, they won a Title after many barren years when they imported a brilliant but controversial foreigner. They have a proud anti-capital, anti-Establishment tradition and have attracted immigrant support throughout the decades.

Cons: However appealing the Club may be, the nature of the city is entirely un-Mancunian. Run by the Camorra, it is utterly corrupt; the unemployment rate is 50% and its filthy streets are stuffed with black marketeers, drug addicts, wide boys and hardline crims. Remind you of anywhere we know? The Liverpudlian parallel is completed thus: Naples is hated by the rest of Italy for its exported thieving, scrounging and violence. Verdict: are you Scousers with a tan?

AC MILAN

Pros: Obviously, their trophy cabinet glitters every bit as brightly as ours. Their stadium is surely the Old Trafford of Italy and they're as loaded as we are. Both our chairmen would get on, being unpopular, naff, right-wing millionaires. And they too date their renaissance from a thrilling bounce-back from the Second Division.

Cons: Don't be fooled by the glorious memories of their Dutch trio. Generally speaking, they have always played the sort of dull, efficient, pressing-game football with relentless offside that conjures up visions of Arsenal, Liverpool and Rovers at their most passion-less. The chairman is a menace to Europe, let alone Italy. As for Milan the city, it is full of the most snotty, racist and tedious breadheads in Italy, set in a region that is far too much like Yorkshire. No thanks.

INTER MILAN

No pros whatsoever. Long before Signor Morratti arrived, they were loathsome enough as it was. When AC signed their delightful Dutchmen, Inter responded by picking up three of Germany's most charmless cynics and played host to Klitmann's theatrics. They invented catenaccio in the 60s, almost destroying football as an art form, and became a byword throughout Europe for bribery, intimidation and negativity – a Continental Leeds. Only good deed ever: bribed a ref to secure Euro semi win over Liverpool in 1965.

SAMPDORIA

No tradition, grotty ground, shit fans and bald centre-forward .... next!

TORINO

Although they lost a superb Title-winning side in the Superga air crash in 1949 which would make for a good emotional link with us, their singular lack of success or style since rules them out. Worse, their fans like to boast that they are the 'true team of Turin' and claim all Juve's fans are out-of-towners. Their general bitterness has attracted City fans in droves, who have rather pathetically formed a Toro Club in Moss Side. That in itself would be enough to drive us into the arms of my choice:

JUVENTUS

Admittedly our clash in 1984 was not exactly good for Anglo-Italian relations and their owner is even dodgier than ours but in every other way they're made for us. Steeped in real tradition with a heaving trophy room, they can claim to be our only rivals in terms of world-wide support.

Not only do they maintain a familiar Red-like dominance over their Bittermen city rivals, they also manage to maintain their glamour and appeal even when second-best to the Liverpool-like AC. They've always been prepared to take on the most mercurial of talents and even in the darkest years could always beat the best on their day. Best of all, they do actually hate Liverpool, despite the 'healing Heysel' hype you may have heard. I conclude my case with a final fitting parallel: Juve came out of the doldrums to win the League after signing a genius Frenchman – Eric's great supporter, Michel Platini. Their relationship came to a happy end with a Euro Cup win: we'd settle for some of that. Forza Juve!

(May 94)

Intense concentration as Giggs prepares to blast another corner . . . into the East Lower

Part Six:

'THIS IS THE MODERN WORLD' - 95/96

1. 1994/95: A Season Of Shame?
2. Now Is The Summer Of Our Discontent
3. Fergie's Transfer Targets
4. Clause For Concern
5. Fishy Faxes
6. Fat-Cats Cock-Up League
7. 'Dear Member ...'
8. It Could Be You!
9. The 1995/96 Season Review?

1994-95: A SEASON OF SHAME?

'English football's disgrace'; 'soccer in the gutter'; 'the shame of our national game'; 'scandal, sleaze and corruption' ... on and on it goes, the familiar litany of 1995's football-on-the-front-page events. We've had drugs of all kinds, bungs, bribes, kung-fu and stamping, deaths in car parks, international hooliganism, sexual shenanigans, in fact every possible piece of tabloid-fodder imaginable. All commentators and so-called experts have agreed that the combined effect has set back the English game by years. What was once a bright, shiny happy world of family-fun has been transformed into a dark, corrupting throwback to the bad old days of the 70s and 80s. Well, bollocks to all that.

Even though we at United have suffered the consequences of our own moments in the season of shame, I still have to say that most of this 'bad news' has been absolutely wonderful. Far from being a terrible advert for our game, these scandals and affairs have breathed new life into what was becoming the most tediously sterile football league in Europe. Every time a footballer is caught skinning up, sniffing his win-bonuses or throwing matches, we get a life-affirming reminder that these footballers are real lads, not 'role-model' automatons. Every outbreak of aggro reminds the world that football still belongs to 'us', not the new breed of Johnny-Come-Latelys who are seeking to impose their behavioural quirks on the rest of us. And when top footballers are pictured by the News of the Screws marauding about with strippers and baby oil, they should be congratulated for their commitment to the entertainment of the public.

What do the doom-merchants want, the screeching moralists who lecture us every time someone misbehaves a bit? They are, of course, all fully hooked-up to the family-values, good clean fun, world of 90s football which is loathed by most of us. They claim that the antiseptic, fair-play, all-above-board philosophy will 'save the game' and build a better future. But just how interesting, exciting and attractive would a Premier League full of Gary Linekers be? Where every chairman is honest, every fan a non-swearing saint and every inter-club rivalry a 'friendly' one? If football were to be banished solely to the back pages, never to dominate the front with the latest scandal or sensation, it would die. This game isn't just about what happens on the pitch; it's about everything else surrounding it. And most of that 'everything else' tends to be a bit unsavoury, if not downright criminal.

The Devil has all the best tunes, they say: quite right. It's the bad, the gory, the outrageous that is memorable and thrilling. Here's to more of the same next year, doubly enjoyable if it appals the tabloids and telly.

Let's have Liverpool players overdosing on smack, let's have small towns being razed to the ground by Leeds savages, let's have entire Clubs being exposed as gambling syndicate covers and let's have some really juicy trans-sexual/S & M/bestiality sex scandals involving chairmen, managers and players' mistresses. The more people it puts off football, the better: we don't want those sorts in football anyway. Spoil the good name of English football, don't they Des?

(May 1995)

Cup Final '95: Keano prepares to give Graham Kelly a left-handed message from Eric

NOW IS THE SUMMER OF OUR DISCONTENT ...

... or so 'The Game' imagined as they expected the author to live up to his Fergie-hating tabloid reputation and pen a scathing piece about the summer sales. But as those intelligent enough not to believe what they read in the gutter press would have surmised, treason against our besieged monarch was the last crime Kurt fancied committing, even if Fergie had indeed murdered a couple of footballing princes ...

"Now Is The Summer Of Our Discontent" – and in parts of Manchester's Red three-quarters, Alex Ferguson is about as popular as Richard the Third himself. Old Trafford's Summer Sale has given even Allied Carpets a run for their money: in a trice, a quarter of that immortal Double-winning side has been vapourized. That would be reason enough for much breastbeating and teeth-gnashing from despondent Reds, especially given that two of the three deportees were at the peak of their career. But add to that the dispiriting, confidence-shattering effect that United's handling of the 'crisis' has had on fans and you have a recipe for revulsion rather than mere regret.

We were not, after all, in the best of summer moods to start with: the loss of the Double already had us on a downer. All we wanted was a nice, quiet summer watching the cricketers at the other Old Trafford conquer all, safe in the knowledge that with injuries healed and suspensions served, a full-strength team led by Cole and Cantona would soon be back to wreak vengeance. Instead we've watched open-mouthed as a maelstrom has engulfed us, causing us as much grief as anything that happened during the season itself.

As is sadly habitual these days, United as a Club have blundered their way through all this with the lack of aplomb you'd expect from an organization without any conception of modern public relations skills. At the height of the fighting, the manager was away on his hols, leaving the chairman to flounder about with his foot in his mouth; then, when Ferguson returned ostensibly to calm tempers and explain all, he had within seven days managed to drive both Ince and Andrei to spill some devastating beans to the tabloids. In truth, the credibility of the Club's public pronouncements had long since been shot to pieces during the initial skirmishes; little wonder, then, that some Reds were now prepared to trust in the players', rather than Club's, version of events. It didn't help the Club's image that the chairman should have opined along the way that United fans had no right to sound off about such matters – his proclamation that we were all just customers paying at the gate with no rights to any other consideration did not, to put it mildly, go down well with the 130,000 who pay to be MEMBERS of MUFC and thus expect to be treated as such.

It's now a matter of public record that the transfers of Ince and Andrei – and, allegedly, to a lesser extent Hughesy's – were a product of personality clashes between manager and player. Few now pretend to believe that the loss of these players can somehow strengthen United as a footballing outfit – any replacements are almost by definition bound to be inferior substitutes, at least for the time being. Some in Manchester mutter darkly that we'd have done better to lose the manager and keep the players; others talk of Ferguson's Napoleonic Busby complex which has made United a grim autocracy. There are allusions to the King across the water, Bryan Robson, waiting for the call on the other side of the Tees; others talk up the contribution of Brian Kidd, who has now committed himself to United despite the panting courtship from City. United fans have always been split between those who adore Fergie and will follow him to the Thatcheresque abyss ("I want to go on and on and on" said both Maggie and Alex) and those who've harboured suspicions which are now biliously surfacing.

So, as the song goes, let's look on the bright side, if there is one amidst all this end-of-empire gloom. If Ferguson now has a squad that he is personally at ease with, perhaps United as a team will benefit from the improved atmosphere, from the sense of all being 'Fergie's Boys'. Of course, he has gambled this summer but then the readiness to take risks has always been an Alex characteristic – and there was no gamble greater and no success bigger than the purchase of Eric Cantona. And whilst it may be true that Fergie's recent record concerning keeping players happy, 'rotating' personnel in team selection and choosing tactics in Europe looks a little ropey, there is one area in which he has been an unqualified success – the breeding of home-grown youth. Talk to Ferguson these days and you'll never be more than a sentence away from a paean of praise for the Fledglings. He has brought these lads on, brought them into the team and now trusts they will help bring home the trophies. It's another gamble, of course: Nicky Butt is not yet a Paul Ince, nor Paul Scholes a Mark Hughes. But as any Red will confirm, there's nothing to match the thrill of watching kids grow into men and from there into stars. If the spirit of Busby and his Babes really is informing everything Ferguson does, it has no less an effect on the fans too; if, come May. the goals of Beckham, Scholes and Butt, defended by the Nevilles, are bringing silverware to Old Trafford then much of this summer's farrago will be forgiven. If not, then the sight of the Guvnor, Andrei and Sparky in alien-coloured shirts will remain grit in Red eyes for a long time to come.

(First published in 'The Game', Aug. 95)

© Drastic, 1995; first published here.

FERGIE'S TRANSFER TARGETS?

With £10 million in the bank, not a day goes by without some new frenzied speculation about who might be coming into Old Trafford. Bearing in mind the fates of Ince, Andrei and Hughesy, players keen to come here have got to fit the ideal Fergie Boy identikit. We look at some of the contenders and rate their chances.

MARC LEGOVERMARS

Current Club: Flash Liquid Rotterdam

Price: £10 million

Plus points: The only available winger in the cosmos.

Young enough to pass himself off as a Fergie Fledgling and thus be immune from criticism.

Long name good for income from shirt-letters.

Speaks enough English to avoid falling victim to the Fergie excuse "I couldna understand him so I didna know he hated my guts/had a hernia/ had the Mafia after him.

Drawbacks: Has mixed with a lot of black players in Holland – might have picked up too many "I'm the Guvnorisms" for Fergie's tastes.

The Dutch have a record of answering back to managers, so unlikely to enjoy the "If You Speak, You're Sold" team-talk rule.

ROBERTO BAGLADY

Current Club: AC/DC Milan

Price: £15.5 million

Plus points: Buddhist philosopher – will make Fergie think he's another Cantona. Religious prohibition on gambling means no running up quarter-million debts that have to be met by leaving for a signing-on fee.

Girly looks and pony-tail locks have Commercial Department slavering.

Drawbacks: Penalty record worse than Choccy's.

Wages demands necessitate building of new tier to finance.

Doesn't shave properly.

Age, over 25, means he could be dumped by Fergie as being over-the-hill at any time however well he was playing.

Speaks Italian which makes it too easy for Signor Morratti to phone him up and say "fancy a lakeside villa?"

HRISTO STICKUP

Current Club: Cruyff's Rejects

Price: £8 million

Plus points: Just the sight of him on the same pitch would be enough to keep Pally flashbackingly awake for the whole game.

He'd be the only player at United with any idea of how to play in Europe – could clue in the management whilst he's at it too.

Wouldn't sulk when dropped like certain ex-winger – misses every other game suspended as it is.

Drawbacks: Going on the Cantona treatment, likely to be under an FA execution order by Christmas.

If he talks to Fergie like he did to Cruyff, likely to be out injured with a "Govan kiss" anyway.

Clearly, none of these is ideal. What we need is a player with all these characteristics: doesn't gamble, doesn't give himself daft nicknames, doesn't object when he's dropped, doesn't answer back or argue, gives 110% in training and in games, if he's black doesn't 'get above his station' in Fergie's eyes, doesn't mess with agents, is prepared to play for months with a double-hernia, doesn't mind being farmed out for sale, brought back, then farmed out again and finally, if possible, will play anywhere the manager asks however shit he is. Got it! – Brian McClair. Forgot Ince, Andrei, Hughes and all them pesky dagos – Choccy is the answer and he's already ours.

(Why doesn't this make me feel any better? In fact, I feel like pegging out. Good job I've got a Donor Card to help others ...)

SUPPORTER'S DONOR CARD

In the event of the death of our Double Double Dream, we would like to help others live on after us. This card gives permission for a doctor – or an agent – to remove the following vital organs and send them to the listed needy recipients:

The heart – to poor Italy

The guts – to West London

The legs – to Merseyside

We will also let the brain go if it has another funny turn.

We do not give permission, however, for the penis to go: it's still in charge.

Signed: Manchester United FC.

(Aug. 95)

CLAUSE FOR CONCERN

The sales of Ince and Kanchelskis in the summer of '95 were controversial enough in themselves but the time-bombs ticking away in the contractual small print threatened to create even more mayhem. The Great Ukrainian War between Goodison and Old Trafford, which at one point promised to wipe many a smug grin off Evertonian faces, brought several dodgy issues to the surface. 'FourFourTwo' asked the author to man the torpedo tubes.

Just when you thought it was safe to dive back into newsprint, here's yet another whinge about Old Trafford's Summer Transfer Circus. However, this time it's the mechanics of deal-making that interests us: the Ince and Andrei transfers came equipped with more bizarre adornments and 'special features' than your average computer game. And laugh all you want at United's serial misfortunes but, as Sir John Hall always tells his grumbling disenfranchised Toons in the INUSA, what happens today at Old Trafford happens everywhere else tomorrow. So what exactly should you have the bullshit-detectors tuned for when a Club ventures into a foreign transfer deal?

In the good old days, paying for players was simple. You parked your whippet outside the selling club's offices, banged a thousand notes in a brown parcel on the desk and said "One Alf Common to take-away please." Nowadays, cash upfront is ridiculously passé: in a universe of the Never-Never, a player is treated like a World of Leather sofa, paid for by instalment over anything up to five years. Paul Ince, for example, has actually cost Inter only £3 million; the rest will supposedly come over the next two summers. (So much for United's mega buying-fund – Martin Edwards' sell-to-buy policy means that United currently have about enough to buy Warren Barton plus a useful First Division reserve, if that's not tautological ...) Wonderful business for the buying club, of course, who can still have funds free for more current spending. Reds meanwhile must also hope that United have remembered to calculate in dollars, not lira: otherwise, given the prospects for the Italian economy, that £3 million balance will be worth about the price of two meat pies by 1997 ... By contrast, domestic transfers under FA regulation must be fully paid-for within the year, with strict limits on the amount to be installed and with moves afoot to make the restrictions even tighter. It's a comparison to hearten the most hardened Eurosceptic. Meanwhile, get ready for the first Eurodeal to be structured like a 25-year mortgage, a concept first pioneered by Big Mal's Manchester City – Marc Overmars sponsored by the Alliance & Leicester?

Another favoured ruse is the series of friendlies between sellers and buyers with the proceeds making up the transfer balance. Again, not a concept very popular in domestic deals but one which Inter Milan in particular seem to love. The Bergkamp matches are at least morally sound as Arsenal fans are asked to cough up the extra readies to buy a player they all want. United fans, however, are expected to pay up over the next two summers in order to finance somebody else's purchase of a player they never wanted to lose. This is chutzpah to be marvelled at but not admired. "Forget the Inter-Toto Cup" sneers Johnny Flacks, veteran campaigner and a leader of the IMUSA, "we're now expected happily to roll up for the Inter-Transfer Trophy. Why should hard-up Reds fork out to make life easier for mega-rich Milanese?" Expect attendances lower than our youth team games for this cynical series.

Both Flacks and Tim Crabbe, the FSA Chair, are united in their contempt for another favourite Eurohit, the secret clause. There's something faintly absurd about footballer's contracts containing hidden codicils – surely this is a device more suited to superpower missile treaties and IRA cease-fire agreements? Yet both the Ince and Andrei deals revealed nasty creatures under the stones when the pressmen got amongst the undergrowth. In Ince's case, it turned out that he had a 12-month escape clause which can't have pleased the Inter tifosi nor any United fan who wants to ensure we get the whole £7 million; Spurs fans won't need any reminding of the fate they suffered thanks to Klinsmann's equivalent clause. A buying Club's loyal fans don't deserve this sort of thing as Crabbe points out: "We're sick and tired of these underhand methods. Clubs demand loyalty of us – we expect the same from them and their servants." Indeed: there's nothing more dispiriting than pouring all your worship into one foreign vessel only to discover he's got a piece of paper saying "if either me or this Club turn out to be crap, I can run straight home to Mummy.

Andrei's transfer, although technically domestic, was virtually a Euro-deal thanks to the overwhelming influence of the previous United-Donetsk arrangement. Here, the semi-secret clauses laid down a monumental signing-on fee for Andrei and a hefty sell-on cut for Donetsk, both of which were news to Reds. No fan can be happy with the knowledge that a star has a standing temptation of a seven-figure bonanza. No wonder Andrei spent most of his Old Trafford days banging in transfer requests. Again, domestically, players cannot reap such upfront windfalls but in the Euro free-for-all, anything goes. And when a player is in trouble with his bookie, drug-dealer, mistress or local mafia, who can resist cashing that winning lottery ticket? As for the sell-on clause, it's all in the context. As Tim Crabbe says "no-one objects to domestic sell-on cuts. It's a lifeline to the minnows and helps the redistribution of wealth." But in a European vista, where the Tinpot Athletics don't figure, such clauses tend "to give too much scope for misunderstanding", as David Meek drily notes. The farrago of the Donetsk cod-fax – "Dear Groovy United: keep the million, we don't really want it, just send us a case of Warrington vodka and we're sorted ..." – demonstrates as much. All this and we haven't even mentioned the dreaded Euro agents yet, that brigade of dodgy Daley-eskis emerging from the wreckage of the Eastern Bloc, armed with knock-off mobiles and Bulgarian bank accounts. It was already bad enough having to cope with the machinations of the FIFA-approved agents ...

Crabbe, Meek and Flacks are all agreed that the time has come for some Euro-wide regulation – for once, being enveloped in Eurocratic red-tape would be welcome. But who is best placed to do the wrapping? Mention UEFA and most fans' leaders run away screaming; the last thing we need is the power-mad gnomes empire-building within our national borders. David Meek, whilst accepting that, for example, a 10% ceiling on signing-on fees would be a nice idea, thinks it unenforceable: "it would be a guarantee of a return to brown paper parcels under the table." Surely there must be some Directorate-General of the European Union who'd love to get stuck in? Oi, Brussels – come and have a go if you think you're hard enough. Please?!

(First published in 'FourFourTwo', Sept. 95)

FISHY FAXES

The one moment of light humour during the summer was the revelation that United had received what is now termed a "cod-fax" concerning Andrei's transfer. A "representative of the player" assured United that it came from the Donetsk vice-president and that it contained a waiver of the £1.1 million cut Donetsk could've claimed from the deal. A week later, a fax arrives from the president saying "where's my f*ckin' money, comrade?" Red faces all round and a three week tug of war with Goodison that threatened to produce the football court case of the year ensued. Now we already knew that those in power at United are often not that bright or worldly-wise but this gullible acceptance of the year's fishiest fax was very heartening. Perhaps we could con United into believing some of the following faxes if we sent them in?

F.A.O.: MUFC Medical Staff
From: Dr. Batson D. Seeling

I write as Mr. Brian McClair's personal physician. I have just examined him and am informing you that he's a bit poorly. In fact, he has both arsey cancer and viral knobbytitis and may not live much longer. I haven't told him yet as I don't want to depress him. I strongly suggest that to avoid contamination of other players you do not let him into Old Trafford ever again and, in view of his limited shelf-life, you should consider selling him immediately. Try Bolton Wanderers, they won't have any players left by November and will be so desperate that they'd even buy Brian.

F.A.O.: Chief Executive, MUFC.
From: De Zoete Welder Merchant Bank, Head Office

We act for our clients, the True Red Consortium consisting of Red Issue and the IMUSA, who wish to buy out your shareholding in MUFC and thus take control of the Board. We assume, judging from the level of salary and dividends you have paid to yourself, that you are as keen as ever to maximise the financial yield from your position at MUFC. We therefore offer £50 million for your holding, which is way above the market rate.

As Blue Chip Merchant Bankers, we can assure you that we have determined that our clients do indeed have such assets and will guarantee they're good for it. Michael Knighton is NOT involved. All we suggest is that we conduct the transaction on your favourite Paul Ince Payment Pattern i.e. you hand over the share deeds now and we'll settle up with you in two years time, honest.

F.A.O. Ken Meritless, Secretary.
From: World Council Of Methodists

We have been watching your splendid career as a part-time lay preacher in our Manchester chapels and feel it is time to offer you the position of Moderator Supreme over all our world churches. You will then be at liberty to inspire hundreds of thousands all over the world with your cries of "Sit down and shut up", "we don't want your sort in here" and your classic "we all love Leeds". We must insist, however, that to give this post your full attention you must resign from your MUFC post and announce that you will never darken Old Trafford's doors again. Yours in sport ...

(Sep. 95)

FAT CATS COCK-UP LEAGUE LATEST - UNITED TOP OF TABLE

It looks as though MUFC are guaranteed one title this year, judging by the brilliant start those who run this Club have made. Forget Cedric Brown at British Gas and the blunderers at North West Water – if you're looking for the biggest six-figure-salary balls-up artists in Britain, Old Trafford's offices contain the champions of '95. Here's their ten highest-scoring incompetencies up to September:

1. Fail to diagnose your star player's double hernia for three months because you think that "all the best medical people are available in Manchester."
2. Allow your manager to remain ignorant of the fact that one of your star players hasn't actually signed his contract.
3. Sell said star player when he's out-of-contract at cut-price when you could've got double the money two months earlier.
4. Allow your greatest player who is "banned from all football activity" to perform against another team without bothering to phone the FA to check first, thus risking the permanent loss of said player.
5. Don't find anything suspicious in a fax handed over by an agent that says "Dear United, we don't want our million pound cut, just send us a couple of crates of vodka."
6. Allow your chairman to go on national radio at a sensitive time and proceed to tell all United fans that "if they don't like it, they can go elsewhere": allow your finance director to tell hard-up Reds on national TV to "go watch the Reserves."
7. Sell your next captain, only ask for £3 million up front, allow him a 12 month escape clause and brand him a traitor thus ensuring he'll never come back and we'll never get the full £7 million for him.
8. Put up ticket prices so much that you struggle to sell the 2,500 extra tickets for routine home games and yet you expect to fill a 55,000 capacity next year.
9. Allow your star striker's doctor to disappear without first finding out if your man is fit to play.
10. ... and finally, give Brian McClair a new contract!

United will have to watch out, however, as City are fast making up ground on us in the cock-up stakes. Meanwhile, marvel at our 'executive leaders', happily raking in mammoth salaries, bonuses and share options – like most companies these days, the process of 'performance-related pay' seems to produce some bloody strange results ...

(Sep. 95)

DEAR MEMBER ...

LMTB and Season Ticket holders will have been delighted to receive that letter from Our Ken at the start of 95/6: but was this the first draft?

There seems to be some confusion as to what is, and is not, acceptable behaviour at Old Trafford. To clarify the position, we set out below our policy.

- Standing for anything other than a goal is NOT ACCEPTABLE

- Singing any song apart from those officially sanctioned by Keith Fane or Ken Merrett is NOT ACCEPTABLE

- Wearing offensive T-shirts i.e. anything not purchased from the Megastore is NOT ACCEPTABLE

- Being, or behaving, like the bloody working class is NOT ACCEPTABLE

The majority of United supporters are people who want to enjoy their visit to Old Trafford in a sterile, church-like atmosphere and do not wish to be disturbed by you proletarian bastards in the cheap seats. We, as a Club, wish to encourage that feeling.

There have been suggestions made that we are opposed to singing or other forms of vocal support. NOTHING COULD BE FURTHER FROM THE TRUTH. We recognize the value of positive support - the players need it and we welcome it. However, chants of "We hate Leeds" (or anyone else for that matter) are not helpful to our players and let us all down. Only the manager is allowed to say "I hate Leeds", "I wish they'd get bloody relegated", "you sheepshagging scum" etc. Do as we say and not as we do.

Towards the end of last season, we received a letter from the Association of Football Families. One paragraph (published below) speaks eloquently of the type of supporter who is an embarrassment to this club and a disease which, if not removed, will fester and drive good, decent people away from the clubs and the sport they love.

"Although we at the Association were pleased with the results of the recent Premier League survey, we are anxious lest it deters clubs from addressing this major problem. There is a minority of "supporters" who don't know how to behave at the modern football ground. They sing throughout the game at the top of their voices in horrid working class accents and sometimes use words like 'sh*t' and 'cr*p'. Some have traces of alcohol on their breath which suggests to us that they have been in a public house that morning rather than church. Some, instead of wearing the nice Club shirts, have T-shirts on that poke cruel fun at our friends from Maine Road and Anfield. We have even experienced these individuals laughing at us because we are carrying twelve Club shop bags or because we sing along to the official Club record. When our members change seats, they still find people like this all around them wherever they go. Sometimes you wonder if these hooligans are in the majority."

This letter is written in a spirit of conciliation and goodwill, even though it might appear we're declaring war on you vermin. We take no pleasure in expelling people from our stadium: however, if we must, we will and we'll be keeping all your season ticket money. Decent, well-behaved supporters are entitled to nothing less. The rest of you are entitled to nothing.

Yours in sport, K.R. Meritless.

(Aug. 95)

IT COULD BE YOU! (not)

There were delighted faces all around the boardroom after the latest Profits Lottery came up trumps for the local Cheshire FatCats Syndicate. "We've hit the £20 million jackpot!" beamed one ex-butcher. The winners, who picked their lucky numbers by using the numbers of their off-shore deposit accounts, benefited from it being a 'roll-over' year: "the pot just got bigger, what with players being sold, ticket prices soaring and no trophy-winning bonuses" explained the syndicate's resident preacher and spiritual guide. Now the only problem they have is how best to screw the fans. *(surely 'spend the booty?' – Ed.)*

"Obviously, we've got to clear this with all the players in our syndicate first" said the leader "but cos me and my best mates paid for most of the tiny original stake back in the beginning, it's really only up to us actually." Their plans for the millions are said to involve the following:

★ Supporting mistresses and second families: £3m

★ Paying for David Weak puff-pieces: £8.35p

★ Extensions to Balearic villas (put in accounts as new training facilities): £2.5m

★ Bribes to keep certain personnel from going to MCFC & Derby: £3m

★ Continued instalment pay-offs to Ukrainian mafia: £5m

★ Treble inflation rate pay increases all-round: £2m

★ Building new MegaExecDoubleBarmaidBlowjob restaurant (Top ten shareholders only) which provides free prawn cocktail and double share option per diner: £1.5m

★ Petty cash balance forward (spending money): the rest

Asked whether they'd continue to play the Lottery despite their win, one syndicate member replied, "Of course: it's great fun, especially when you're guaranteed a jackpot every year..."

(Oct. 95)

THE 1995/96 SEASON?

Before any of us get too excited about the forthcoming season's prospects, read the following. UF PRODUCTIONS employed the services of well-known clairvoyant Pisstake Peg, a woman who successfully predicted the sex of two of her three children before they were born, and somehow can't see us filling our new triple-decker stand. But then again, if she was that bloody clever she'd have won the lottery by now.

AUGUST

Alex Ferguson turns down a £12 million bid for Brian McClair; he says, "While we have Eric Cantona out of action we will need McClair to take the penalties."

Eric Cantona puts in a transfer request after reading Alex Ferguson's new book. Ferguson states he has the ideal replacement in Nicky Butt.

After the first home game of the season, United lose three match balls over the Stretford End, the costs of which are docked from McClair's wages. Nicky Butt is knocked unconscious in the same game by the puff of the referee's whistle as he blows for a throw – in.

After buying a house in Southport, Andrei Kanchelskis is told his transfer to Everton is cancelled because it was his turn to clean the toilets at the changing room and he forgot. Andrei's agent accuses Alex Ferguson of trying to sabotage his plans of becoming an overnight millionaire. Alex Ferguson agrees to make a statement but is taken to hospital after biting through his lip.

Ryan Giggs retires from football to take over from Robbie in Take That.

Paul Parker is decapitated in a horrific gardening accident; club physician David Fevered diagnoses a bad headache and prescribes a dose of aspirin.

Manchester City are bottom of the first published league table of the season.

SEPTEMBER

Alan Ball says there's no need to panic after City lose 7-0 at home to Exeter City in the second round of the League Cup. "We had a chance early in the second half and that gives us something to build on," said Mr Ball. Andrei Kanchelskis is arrested for violent behaviour in the Nat West Bank after he finds out that his cheque for £1.3 million has bounced.

A copy of Alex Ferguson's secret apology to Leeds United is leaked to the press. In it Ferguson claims he was misquoted in saying "I hate Leeds"; he had actually said, "I f*ckin' hate Leeds."

Demand for tickets is such that supporters have to charter helicopters to hover above Old Trafford on match day. Three supporters are killed when a Brian McClair penalty brings down one of the helicopters.

Nicky Butt makes a successful slide tackle in training; later that day Denis Irwin is placed on the transfer list. Alex Ferguson tells reporters, "Nicky Butt is as good a full back as you'll find in the Premiership".

Eric Cantona returns to first team action and scores all nine goals in a convincing win over Liverpool. As the final whistle blows he is charged by the FA of conducting himself in a manner likely to incite a riot. Graham Kelly unveils a new extension to his double chin and tells reporters, "We suspended Cantona from all footballing activities but no sooner has the ban ended then he immediately goes and shows the sort of skills we've been trying to kill in British football for years. He is entirely to blame for the jealous Liverpool fans machine-gunning the family stand as the ninth goal went in ... oh, and Chelsea must also take some of the blame." Mr Kelly then attempts a drop kick on a reporter who asks for some photos of his wife in a bikini. He breaks three concrete slabs and his pelvis as he falls.

OCTOBER

The Director of Public Prosecutions announces his plans to prosecute Eric Cantona for football so skilful that Gary Lineker is provoked into saying, "I wish he'd just f*ck off back to France" live on Match Of The Day.

The Queen announces she is to sell the Crown Jewels to pay for a new shopping arcade in Buckingham Palace. She states that the arcade, which is due to be called The Nicky Butt Precinct, will be as good as any arcade in the country.

Nicky Butt scores eight goals in the local derby with City; he is unfortunately denied a place in the record books by Andy Cole who scores thirty-seven in the same game. City boss Alan Ball says there is no need to panic, as City nearly won a corner in the first half and that is something to build on.

That same week United are knocked out of Europe, losing 1-0 in the away leg. The morning after, photographs are published of David May congratulating the goalscorer and a reporter states May sang "4-0 Barcelona" on the plane all the way home.

The cardboard cut-out season ticket holders of the North Stand voice their anger when it is revealed they are not going to get their old seats back when the new stand is completed. Instead the North Stand is going to be the first all-executive box stand in the country. Tickets will cost £10,000 per season under the title of V.I.P. Executive Incontinent Club Class Double Whopper Half Time Blow Job By A Fit Bar Maid With A Free Programme Box. Hugh Grant becomes the first person to apply for a ticket and Gillian Taylforth enquires about the bar work.

United turn down a £9 million bid from Juventus for Andrei Kanchelskis. Kanchelskis goes on hunger strike.

NOVEMBER

Andrei Kanchelskis is fined by the club when an escape tunnel is discovered under the changing rooms at Old Trafford. Kanchelskis is reported to be distraught, as the tunnel was only five miles short of Italy.

In a show-down meeting with Alex Ferguson, Lee Sharpe asks why he can't play on the left-wing now that Ryan Giggs has left for Take That. Ferguson tells him, "I believe Nicky Butt is as good a left-winger as you'll find in the Premiership".

A Sunday tabloid prints a leaked copy of a letter from club physician David Fevered to his predecessor Jim McGregor in which he asks, "Where do babies come from?"

Graham Kelly announces that Eric Cantona is to be 'banned from all activities' but Eric's wife successfully challenges this in Court. Gary Lineker calls the Judge "a f*cking twat!" live on Match of the Day but he says it in such a mild mannered, nicey-nicey tone of voice that no-one complains.

DECEMBER

Nicky Butt catches a ball in training; later that day Peter Schmeichel is placed on the transfer list. Alex Ferguson tells reporters, "I believe Nicky Butt is as good a goalkeeper as you'll find in the Premiership". Andy Cole's career hangs in the balance when it is revealed he played a full ninety minutes with a multiple fracture of the thigh bone. Club physician David Fevered had diagnosed a mild hamstring and prescribed the magic sponge.

Peter Boyle releases his latest single entitled 'What The F*ck Is Going On?'. It sells no copies at all because it's f*cking awful.

Nelson Mandela sends a message of sympathy to Andrei Kanchelskis.

United accept a £10 million bid for Peter Schmeichel from Juventus but there is uproar when it is revealed that United will get a down-payment of only £10,000 with the balance being paid at £50 per week.

Ryan Giggs is sacked from Take That for refusing to hold the microphone in his right hand.

Eric Cantona attacks another camera-man. He is wrestled away by Alex Ferguson and told to get on with the game. Match of the Day repeat the incident a record 32,000 times. Gary Lineker calls for him to be publicly castrated, with blunt shears and no anaesthetic.

JANUARY

The ball hits Nicky Butt on the head in training; later that day Gary Pallister is put on the transfer list. Alex Ferguson tells reporters, "I believe Nicky Butt is as good a central defender as you'll find in the Premiership". To cover against any lack of experience in defence that this may cause, Ferguson offers Steve Bruce a new eight-year contract.

United accept a £10 million bid from Juventus for Pallister but this time they insist on cash. The transfer is followed by an Emergency General Meeting of Shareholders who vote by a majority of 51% to pay a dividend of £10 million to chairman Martin Edwards to secure his services for the next six months. United also use this opportunity to announce an increase in 75% in the cost of 1996/97 LMTBs; this is to cover the building costs af a new SuperDuper Mega-Whopper Store by the entrance to the North Stand.

United accept an offer for Andrei Kanchelskis from Man City. Kanchelskis releases a statement: "I want to play for Mr Ferguson – he is a wonderful, kind and generous man".

Gary Lineker announces he is to have a sex change. "I've always wanted to be a man," he tells reporters.

FEBRUARY

Gary Lineker's sex change operation fails when the willy rejects him.

More trouble for United physician David Fevered when photographs of Paul Parker's decapitated and decomposing body are printed by a Sunday tabloid. "I thought that was Robbie Fowler," he tells reporters. Alex Ferguson spots Nicky Butt combing his hair in the mirror; confused by seeing both Butt and his reflection, he puts Nicky Butt on the transfer list. He tells reporters, "I believe Nicky Butt is as good a Nicky Butt as you'll find in the Premiership."

Nicky Butt is taken into hospital suffering from stress. He tells reporters, "I can't take all this pressure. I'm just a kid."

Mark Hughes is named P.F.A. Player of the Year for a record third time.

Claims that Halley's Comet have been spotted in the skies are refuted by

NASA, who put the phenomenon down to one of Brian McClair's penalties re-entering the earth's atmosphere.

Man City fans, fearing relegation, start a "Bring Back Peter Swales" campaign.

Andrei Kanchelskis returns from international duty stating he is unfit for domestic action due to a recurrence of the mysterious belly problem – and the lack of 1.3 million quid.

MARCH

A Sunday tabloid reveals that United, who have played all season without a right winger, have made a secret bid to The Dog and Duck of three cans of Boddies for their reserve winger Ralph Milne. The Dog and Duck reply that they'll consider a player swap with Nicky Butt, as they're looking for a junior glass collector. Due to injuries, decapitations and transfers, United have to play the return game with Man City with only two players, Eric Cantona and Nicky Butt. City escape with a draw when Nicky Butt scores an own goal. The atmosphere at Old Trafford decreases to such a level that club secretary Ken Merrett sends all members a letter which states, "please ... sing We All F*ckin Hate Leeds."

Ralph Milne rejects the chance to join United; he tells reporters, "F'ckin Hell, it's bad enough being Ralph Milne."

Panic in the Old Trafford camp leads Eric Cantona to release a statement: "But for the woodwork in the final game of last season at West Ham, and the crossbar in the Cup Final, we would again be double winners. Let's become a team again." Nicky Butt joins him in the press conference and tells reporters, "When the trawlers are full of sardines, there will be lots of budgies with tin openers." Brian McClair shouts from the back of the room that he understands what he is saying.

Francis Lee tells reporters that Alan Ball's job is as safe as houses.

APRIL

Man City sack Alan Ball as their manager. Francis Lee is reminded of his recent comment but claims he was talking about a Barratt house.

United are neck and neck in the race for the Premiership (well, what did you expect? Nicky Butt's not as bad as he looks, you know). Ferguson fails in a £6 million bid to bring back Mark Hughes so he can drop him for the final few important games.

The FA ban Eric Cantona for the remainder of the season. They tell a packed press conference, "We'll come up with a reason later".

Brian Kidd joins Man City as manager. Alex Ferguson appoints Nicky

Butt as his new assistant; he tells reporters, "I believe Nicky Butt is as good an assistant manager as you'll find in the Premiership."

United reach the Cup Final; Andrei Kanchelskis announces that his mysterious belly problem has mysteriously cleared up and he will be fit for the final.

Club physician David Fevered is rushed into hospital suffering from a drugs overdose when he mistakes a tub of paracetomol for a tube of Smarties.

MAY

United lose the Cup Final after fielding a team consisting only of Brian McClair, who is taken off early in the second half after missing a penalty

Middlesbrough pip United for the Championship and make a successful bid for Eric Cantona.

Paul Ince wins European Footballer of the Year.

Martin Edwards buys Alaska from America.

Alex Ferguson transfer lists his kidneys which he publicly accuses of being past it.

Juventus win the European Cup with a team consisting mostly of United's double winning players. They announce their plans to buy Mark Hughes for the start of the following season.

United announce they are to withdraw from competitive football to concentrate on their merchandising business.

(By UF Productions, first published in 'Red Issue' Aug. 95)

– THE END –

MAD ABOUT

Sigma Leisure has a small but growing list of football books, including – gasp! – two about Manchester City and a forthcoming "A to Z" of Stoke City. We also publish books on walking, cycling & local heritage – so there's a Sigma book for *any* Saturday in the year!

RED FEVER!

FROM MANCHESTER TO RIO AS UNITED SUPPORTERS – Steve Donoghue
(£7.95)

A hilarious account of a United fan who travelled the world to support his team. Large format, fully illustrated plus colour section!

MANCHESTER!

If you enjoyed "Despatches from Old Trafford", you'll love UNITED WE STOOD – the book that shot Richard Kurt straight to the top of the best-seller lists! Essential reading for all true Reds, and a good laugh for everybody else (except followers of Man City, Leeds etc etc)!

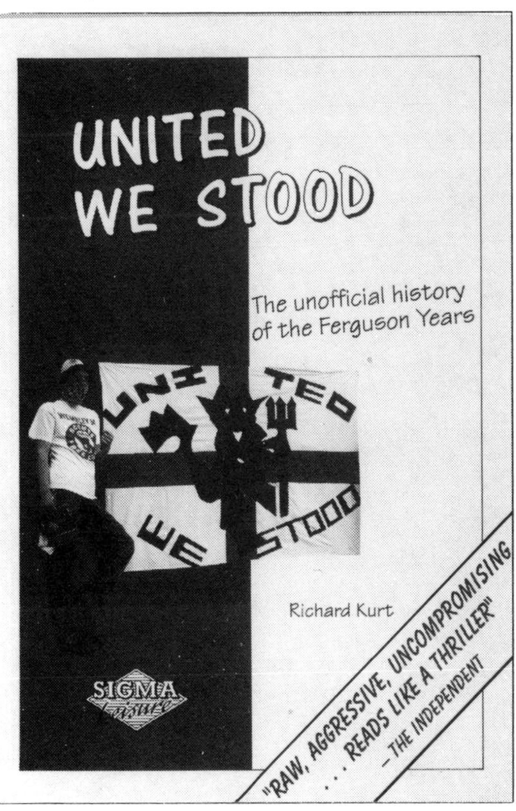

UNITED WE STOOD

– THE UNOFFICIAL HISTORY OF THE FERGUSON YEARS

– Richard Kurt

(£6.95)

If easily offended by cutting remarks about the opposition, unkind (but hilarious) cartoons and colourful language, don't buy this book – but for entertainment and incisive analysis, open your wallets now!